Triumph
of the
Hero

Triumph
of the
Hero

GREEK AND ROMAN MYTH

MYTH AND MANKIND

TRIUMPH OF THE HERO: Greek and Roman Myth
Writers: Tony Allan (The Time of the Hero,
When Men Were Giants, The Trojan Tragedy,
The Legacy of the Heroes)
Piers Vitebsky (Quests and Trials, The Heroes Come Home)
Consultant: Dr Michael Trapp, King's College London

Created, edited and designed by
Duncan Baird Publishers
Castle House
75–76 Wells Street
London W1P 3RE

DUNCAN BAIRD PUBLISHERS
Managing Editor: Diana Loxley
Managing Art Editor: Gabriella Le Grazie

Series Editor: Christina Rodenbeck
Editors: Charles Phillips, David Gould
Designers: Christine Keilty, Gail Jones
Picture Researcher: Anne-Marie Ehrlich
Editorial Researcher: Clare Richards
Editorial Assistant: Jessica Hughes

Artworks: Alan McGowan
Map Artworks: Lorraine Harrison
Artwork Borders: Iona McGlashan

TIME-LIFE BOOKS
Staff for TRIUMPH OF THE HERO: Greek and Roman Myth
Editorial Manager: Tony Allan
Design Consultant: Mary Staples
Editorial Production: Justina Cox

Published by Time-Life Books BV, Amsterdam

First Time-Life English language printing 1998

TIME-LIFE is a trademark of
Time Warner Inc, USA

ISBN 0 7054 3573 3

Colour separation by Colourscan, Singapore
Printed and bound by Milanostampa, SpA, Farigliano, Italy

Title page: Theseus flings the giant Sinis from a pine tree.
This red-figure bowl dates from 490BC.
Contents: The handsome features of Pericles, one of
the historical heroes of Athens and a founding father
of democracy, were captured by a sculptor in this
bust dated around 499–429BC.

30 29 28 27 26 25 24 23 22 21 20 19 18 17 16 15 14 13 12 11 10 9 8 7 6 5 4 3 2

Contents

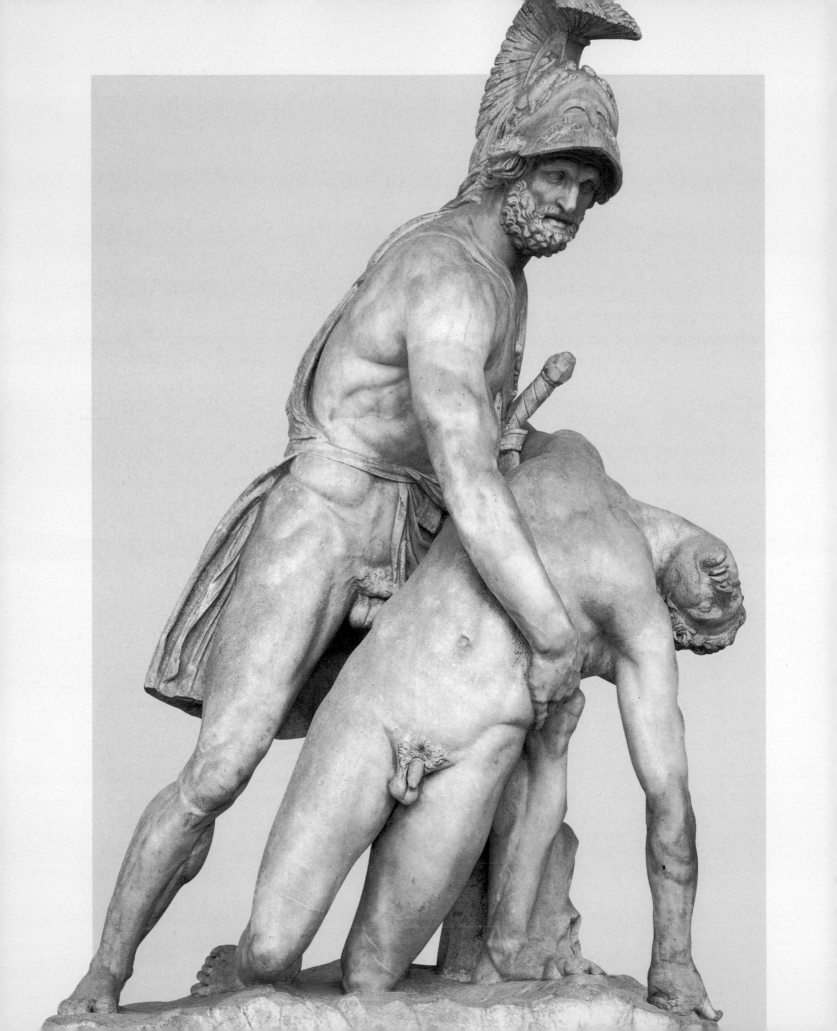

THE TIME OF THE HERO

Halfway through Homer's great epic the *Odyssey*, the hero Odysseus finally makes his way back to his island kingdom of Ithaca after an absence of twenty years. In that time he has endured all the horrors of the Trojan War and suffered great hardship on a protracted journey home. He has beaten off giants, escaped from enchantments and even resisted the lure of the Sirens' sweet songs. Yet he does not return in triumph or in a blaze of glory. Instead he comes to his own door disguised as a beggar. For time has passed and he has been all but forgotten by his people. His palace is filled with a crowd of hostile strangers. The only creature to recognize him in his suit of rags is his old dog.

The story ends happily, with Odysseus revealing his true identity and reclaiming what belongs to him. Yet the downbeat tone of the return says much about the Greek hero myths and helps explain their enduring appeal. If Odysseus, Achilles and Heracles are still familiar names today it is because they were far more than muscular supermen. The Greek heroes invariably had great strength and valour; yet they also revealed frailties, and like the rest of humankind they were subject to the vagaries of unpredictable fate. No other people had as many hero myths as the Greeks, perhaps because none had such a high conception of human potentiality; it was a Hellenic trait to attribute to mortals astonishing feats and remarkable qualities that in other cultures would have been the prerogatives of the distant gods. Yet the Greeks were also realists, and they accepted that their heroes' very humanity exposed them to the risks of divine disfavour, occasional defeat and the inescapable physical decline of old age.

Over the centuries, this combination of qualities has proved lastingly attractive. First the Romans took over the myths lock, stock and barrel, even adding a hero of their own in the shape of Aeneas, a minor player in the Trojan War who became the legendary founder of Rome; and from them the stories joined the cultural heritage of the Western world. Along the way the tales lost none of their power to excite and to surprise listeners and readers; Theseus and Jason are as at home in the computer age as they were when illiterate bards sang of their deeds by the light of torches.

Above: Like mortals, the heroes had to overcome doubt and fear in facing an unknowable future – both on their travels and in battle. In this 5th-century BC relief, soldiers prove their courage in combat.

Opposite: The warrior Menelaus drags the corpse of Patroclus behind the Greek battle lines. This incident in the Trojan War marked the beginning of the end of the nine-year siege.

The Aegean Dawn

In the beginning, there was the land. The roots of classical mythology lie deep in the soil of Greece, and the character of the tales, like that of the Greek people themselves, was shaped by the country's peculiar geography. The interior is mountainous, covered for much of its extent by the southernmost outreach of the Balkan massif. Plains suitable for arable farming are few and far between. Instead there are valleys, cut off from one another by ranges that everywhere act as barriers to communication. Such an environment encourages political fragmentation. For most of its history, ancient Greece was an accumulation of rival enclaves, united by language, religion and culture but divided by almost everything else.

The first farmers may have started trying to scratch a living from this ungenerous region as early as 7000BC, living in edgy coexistence with hunter-gatherers who pursued game in the hills, at that time densely forested. Little is known of these Stone Age populations except that they buried their dead under the floors of their houses. Linguistic evidence suggests they were not Greek-speaking, though they were to bequeath to later residents a heritage of place names, as well as a residue of terms with non-Greek roots, including the names for "fig", "bean", "cypress" and "sea".

They also gave them terms for the vine and the olive, both of which were developed from plants that grew wild in the region. By about 3000BC these staples had spread across the land, bringing something of an economic revolution in their wake. For wine and olive oil were exportable commodities, and trade blossomed as their use spread – with dramatic effects for the population. Studies of habitation patterns in the Peloponnese, the 21,500-square-kilometre peninsula that makes up the south of mainland Greece, suggest that in its vine- and olive-growing districts the number of

settlements increased by a factor of five between 4000 and 2500BC. In the north of the country, where cereals remained the principal crop, growth proceeded at a tenth of that rate.

A similar revolution was taking place on the islands that between them make up almost a fifth of the country. One group in particular stood out. Settled from at least 4000BC and possibly long before, the Cyclades in the southern Aegean Sea underwent much the same process of development as the Peloponnese 200 kilometres to the east.

From early on, the islanders looked to sea-trade to supply goods and raw materials that could not be produced locally. Even before the coming of the new agriculture, they had exported pottery, stone vases and dark, glass-like obsidian, used to

Craftsmen from the Cycladic islands won fame for their work in clay and stone. This decorative object in the shape of a woman's womb is from Syros, *c*.2500BC. It may have been a fertility symbol.

make knives and scrapers. There was also a lively market for the distinctive Cycladic stone figurines, whose smooth curves and blank features were to influence a number of twentieth-century artists including Modigliani and Brancusi.

The islanders' geographical isolation protected them from a wave of disruption that affected the mainland in the years before 2000BC. Archaeological evidence indicates that at that time many long-standing settlements were sacked and burned. The destruction seems to have been connected with the arrival of a new wave of settlers from the north. The newcomers spoke an Indo-European tongue that was to form the basis of the future Greek language. They also brought with them a new style of pottery and, most likely, horses and the skills of horsemanship.

Scholars still argue over whether these incomers – cousins of other groups who were making their way towards western and northern Europe and to the Indian sub-continent at roughly the same time – came as invaders or as peaceful infiltrators, taking advantage of the troubles in the Greek lands to find a new home. Either way, they stayed and Greece changed with their coming. At first the results were mostly negative. The early centuries of the second millennium were a benighted period in which housing designs reverted to a more primitive type and villages needed walls to protect them against marauders.

Meanwhile changes of a more promising kind were afoot in the Aegean, and they were to leave a lingering imprint on Greek mythology. The

Forbidding mountains, rocky landscapes and sweeps of glittering blue sea – here seen from a coastal plain on the island of Crete – shaped the imagination of the Greek myth-makers.

9

island of Crete had been inhabited since at least the seventh millennium and had been trading with Egypt since 3000BC. Some time around the start of the second millennium it blossomed, perhaps because of wine and olive production but now also metallurgy, which was spreading through the region. Traders set out in high-prowed wooden ships plying the seas between Greece, the Levant and Egypt with cargoes of timber, olive oil, wine, pottery and metalwork. Cretan colonies formed in the Cyclades, on the Greek mainland and in Asia Minor.

The wealth generated by this burgeoning activity found its way back to the Cretan capital of Knossos, where a vast palace was first laid out in about 1900BC. This was the home of Minos – probably a generic royal title like "pharaoh" rather than the name of an individual king. The structure was elegant and sophisticated, unlike any previous royal residence. Its walls were decorated with brilliant frescoes and amenities included the Mediterranean world's first known system of indoor plumbing. Most surprisingly, the whole complex had no defensive walls: masters of the waves, the Cretans evidently felt secure enough in their island stronghold to go without fortification.

For 500 years, the Cretans dominated the eastern Mediterranean, gradually eclipsing the earlier Cycladic culture of the islands. They also had a profound influence on the mainland, which borrowed pottery styles from them along with the arts of bronze-making and of writing, for Minoan scribes had developed a still largely undeciphered script, known to modern scholars as Linear A.

Yet despite the extent of the debt, relations – to judge from later mythology – were not always friendly. The familiar story of Theseus and the Minotaur (see pages 50–55) has the Cretans demanding a tribute of young Athenian men and

The production of metal objects such as this double-headed axe of *c.*1500BC was an activity at which the Cretans of the Minoan period excelled. But the island's civilization was not a warlike one; its prosperity and wide influence were based on trade.

women for sacrifice to the monster; and tales of the Labyrinth in which the man bull lived most likely reflected the amazement of provincially minded mainlanders at the maze-like complexity of the Knossos palace (see page 55).

The Warlord Era

Yet things were changing in continental Greece, too. From about 1650BC, parts of the mainland began to look outward to a wider world. By that time the Indo-European incomers had intermingled with the native peoples to create the race that Homer was to call Achaean, and it found a political centre at Mycenae in the eastern Peloponnese.

Here the 19th-century German archaeologist Heinrich Schliemann discovered five royal burial chambers, each set at the bottom of shafts between five and eight metres deep. Besides the bones of their occupants, they contained a fortune in grave goods. There were amber beads from the Baltic, silver from Anatolia, glass and alabaster from Crete and gems from the Middle East, alongside gold vessels and ornaments of many kinds. Although Schliemann himself believed he had found the tomb of the legendary 12th- or 13th-century ruler Agamemnon (see page 15), the graves are now known to be much earlier, dating from between 1600 and 1500BC. Their riches were evidence of wider trading connections in that early era than scholars had hitherto dared to imagine.

Mycenae itself was one of a number of similar kingdoms, each ruled by a warrior aristocracy,

The Secrets of Knossos

Apart from vague memories of King Minos in Greek myth, all knowledge of the great Bronze Age civilization of Crete was lost even by Homer's day. It was only rediscovered in the years after 1900 by an English scholar who stumbled on the remains of the royal palace at Knossos.

Arthur Evans was a wealthy collector who served as Keeper of the Ashmolean Museum in Oxford. In his pursuit of antiquities, he became interested in a class of small carved seals that he was offered by dealers on mainland Greece and in the Aegean islands. Besides elegantly engraved scenes of hunting and sea-life, some of the tiny objects appeared to bear short inscriptions in an unknown form of writing.

The primary source seemed to be Crete, so Evans travelled to the island in 1894 to find out where the dealers might be unearthing the objects. There he soon became intrigued by a large mound at Knossos that was rumoured to contain ruins. It took several years for him to get permission to undertake an excavation, but he finally began digging there in 1900.

What he found took his breath away and became his life's passion. He continued work on the site until 1935, by which time he had uncovered a vast palace containing several hundred rooms, some decorated with animated frescoes, others lined with storage jars almost two metres high. There were also many clay tablets inscribed in the script that had originally drawn him to the island and which he christened Linear A. Taken together, his discoveries were enough to reveal to the world the existence of a totally forgotten civilization.

A fresco from the palace at Knossos, *c.*1500BC, presents a stylized image of ladies from the royal court.

but it seems in time to have exerted a fragile over-lordship over the region. For this reason, and also because it was the first to be discovered, it has given its name to the entire culture. The term also denotes an epoch in Aegean history. For in the course of the next two centuries, the newly domi-nant Mycenaeans wrested control of the eastern Mediterranean from Crete.

They were helped by a string of natural disasters that devastated the island. Archaeological evidence indicates that the palace at Knossos was destroyed by an earthquake around 1600BC. That time it was rebuilt and flourished again. But 150 years later the explosion of the volcanic island of Thera (today's Santorini), a Cretan colony just 110 kilometres to the north, seems to have done last-ing economic damage. A tsunami, or series of tidal waves, was driven across the sea by the explosion and may have swamped Crete's north coast, taking out most of the fleet on which the island's wealth depended. A blanket of volcanic ash is thought to have descended on the eastern half of the island, devastating its agriculture.

Any account of the cataclysm has to be qualified with the words "maybe" and "perhaps", as no written records survive; modern seismolo-gists have deduced the damage from Santorini's shattered remnants. What is certain is that, although Minoan Knossos survived for some decades afterwards, it never regained its pre-emi-nence. Inscriptions in Linear B – which unlike its predecessor Linear A was an early form of Greek – are found on Crete from about 1450BC onwards. Their presence suggests that Mycenaeans took advantage of Crete's misfortunes to seize control. Around 1400BC, the Knossos palace was razed a second time. It remained buried for 3,300 years – until English archaeologist Arthur Evans dug it up.

The continental culture that supplanted the Minoan civilization had until that time been very much in its thrall; mainland pottery and other arte-facts showed no trace of originality until after the collapse of Knossos. Yet it quickly turned out to have a marked character of its own. One of its defining features was a sense of insecurity that had no parallel on Minoan Crete. There, palaces had stood unprotected, but in continental Greece rulers sheltered behind massive walls.

The defences were all too necessary, for the Mycenaean world was a thoroughly unsafe place. A new class of warrior prince wielded bronze swords and swept into battle on chariots; in fact the first known Greek representation of a chariot appears on a headstone topping one of the Myce-naean shaft graves.

The new society's militarism had its roots in profound changes in combat technology. The

Boxers square up in a 16th-century BC fresco from the Cycladic island of Santorini. Some writers claim the island – whose volcano may have dealt a fatal blow to the Minoan civilization of Crete – as a site for the mythical kingdom of Atlantis.

The following labels appear on the map:

Thrace
Troy • Troad
Mysia
Thessaly
Lemnos
Magnesia
AEGEAN SEA
Phthia •
Lydia
Locris •
Phocis •
Skyros
Thebes •
Ithaca
Attica
Cephallenia
Corinth •
Elis
Salamis • Athens
Caria
Zacynthus
Mycenae •
Argos •
Arcadia
Naxos
Lycia
Pylos •
Sparta •
Knossos •
Crete

Bronze Age Greece

The warlike Mycenaeans of Bronze Age Greece dominated the entire Aegean. Later generations gave lasting fame to the kingdoms and cities of the era, making them the sites for the exploits of great mythical heroes. The boundaries of the kingdoms can only be drawn approximately as their exact dimensions remain a matter of dispute for scholars.

bronze of which swords, shields and armour were now made was a rare and expensive commodity that only a wealthy elite could afford. The same applied to the horses used to pull the war chariots. Economic exigency helped create a military aristocracy that could use its monopoly of the most powerful instruments of war to impose its will on the rest of the population. Unlike the chariot-borne rulers of the Near East, however, the Mycenaeans also took to the sea. Their ships gave them control over Crete and enabled them to gather from far and wide the great wealth evident from the shaft graves. In exchange for locally produced hides, timber, wine and olive oil, the boats brought back gold and silver, tin, copper and ivory, along with papyrus on which records could be kept in the proto-Greek Linear B script.

Additional wealth no doubt also came from raiding, for there is no reason to suppose that the Mycenaeans became any less warlike when they took to the waves. Much of the wealth gained by trade and piracy found its way back to the fortress-palaces, whose rulers needed a constant supply of treasure to reward loyal vassals and placate uncertain allies. Even so, enough affluence passed to the population as a whole for settlements to spread faster than they had done for the past millennium.

This aristocratic Bronze Age world was crucial to the hero myths of ancient Greece; it is no exaggeration to say that all the great sagas of Heracles and Jason and Theseus and Troy had their roots in folk-memories of the Mycenaean civilization. The myths themselves make the derivation clear by specifically linking the heroes to important Bronze Age sites like Thebes and Tiryns. Significantly, some of these had shrunk into insignificance in the later era when the myths were written down, and could only owe their prominent part in the stories to memories of the distant past.

For after three centuries of dominance, the Mycenaean civilization with all its splendours disappeared into a Dark Age whose coming has never been fully explained. The first inkling of trouble came at the start of the thirteenth century, when pharaonic Egypt fell from a golden age into a long period of economic decline. The tide of prosperity receded across the Mediterranean world, leaving the region's populations hungry and restless. Vassal princes became fractious as their overlords had less largesse to offer.

In response, Mycenae's rulers reacted in the only way they knew, by stepping up the pace of military activity. Fear and uncertainty increased. It was at this time that labourers put up the great defensive walls that stand in ruins today; at Tiryns, the bulwarks are in places fifteen metres thick.

As the pressures of economic recession squeezed a swollen population, marauding bands took to arms to secure a living. Soon whole tribes were on the move. Sometime around the year 1200BC the Hittite empire, which had dominated Anatolia for over 300 years, collapsed under the onslaught. Then in 1186BC, raiders known to history as the Sea Peoples attacked Egypt itself, only to be driven back by Pharaoh Ramses III in an epic naval battle fought at the mouth of the Nile.

This was the historical backdrop against which was fought the semi-legendary Trojan War – the focal point for the entire mythological Age of Heroes. Ever since Heinrich Schliemann's excavations at Troy in the 1870s (see pages 104–107), it

Warriors of the Mycenaean age loom larger than life in the Greek hero myths. The clash of Achilles and Hector before the walls of Troy is depicted on this 4th-century BC altarfront.

The tomb of the once great Agamemnon in Mycenae is a reminder that glory fades. The Greek myths gave new life to the glorious past – in the face of decline. By the time that Homer sang of Agamemnon and Mycenae, the real city had become an impoverished backwater, long eclipsed by its neighbour, Argos.

has been recognized that there is at least a possibility that Mycenaean forces did indeed sack the city around the year 1184BC, the date traditionally assigned for the event in classical times.

If so, the assault must have been their swansong, for thereafter the Dark Age descended in earnest on the Greek world. Populations declined, trade dried up, and economic life retracted to village or subsistence level. Culture became impoverished, and knowledge of writing was lost; when literacy returned to Greece, it came via an entirely new alphabet, no longer Cretan in inspiration but rather a North Semitic script adapted from the Phoenicians that remains the basis of most Western writing systems.

In later times, the Greeks themselves associated this period of catastrophic decline with the incursion of the Dorians, Greek-speakers from the northern border regions. Such people undoubtedly existed, for in classical times their descendants were still recognizable by their distinctive accents. But modern scholars disagree as to whether the Dorians came as conquering invaders or peaceful infiltrators. Proponents of the first view cite archaeological evidence for widespread destruction in virtually all the major Mycenaean centres in the course of the twelfth century

BC. Their opponents suggest that the Greek world imploded, and that the sacking and burning was the result of civil war or infighting between separate Mycenaean powers; according to this view, the Dorians were opportunistic incomers, driven southwards by hostile incursions of northern peoples into their own territories, who took advantage of the general chaos to establish themselves through much of the Greek mainland.

Whatever the truth, their arrival coincided with a technological change that was to have profound effects for the warrior heroes of the late Bronze Age. This was the introduction of iron, which first appeared in Anatolia in about 1400BC but only came into widespread use after the destruction of the Hittite empire. In the last two centuries of the second millennium, knowledge of iron-smelting techniques spread around Europe and by 1000BC it had become the principal material from which weapons and tools were made.

In terms of quality, iron had few advantages over bronze, especially as it was prone to rust. But it was cheaper. Iron ores were plentiful, and ploughs and sickles made of the new metal were soon within the reach of every substantial farmer.

The effects on warfare were equally profound. Iron democratized the battlefield – once

15

A Fresh Beginning

The combined effects of economic contraction and pressure from the Dorians drove many Greeks to seek a better future overseas, sparking a wave of emigration that was to continue for almost 500 years. For protection in unfamiliar, potentially hostile lands, the settlers went in groups, just as the *Mayflower* pilgrims to America were to do two and a half millennia later; and like the New England pioneers, these travelling communities took their own culture with them. From possibly as early as 1000 until about 550BC, little bits of Greece were planted overseas, from the Black Sea to the western Mediterranean.

Although the colonies remained passionately Greek in culture and attitude, they nonetheless were forced to devise novel arrangements to meet the challenges of life in new lands. Sited perilously behind hastily constructed walls on promontories and in other easily defensible locations, they quickly developed a spirit of experiment and innovation that could hardly have arisen in the long-settled lands back home, where people naturally looked to the past for guidance. This sentiment was particularly evident in the settlements of Ionia on the coast of west-central Asia Minor, which looked across the Aegean to Athens as their homebase. It was in Ionian communities like Miletus, Ephesus and Colophon that the concept of the city-state was born; spreading back to the mainland, it would become the emblem of Greece's classical age.

Ancient tradition also described Homer as Ionian, and the language and content of the *Iliad* and the *Odyssey* both suggest that it was indeed in Ionia that they were first put into writing. But almost nothing is known of the poet's life, if indeed he ever existed; one body of scholarly opinion insists that there never was such a man

whole ranks and battalions of soldiers could be provided with metal armour and weapons, the warrior elite lost much of its intrinsic advantage. The future was to lie with ranks of infantry capable of withstanding chariot charges. Henceforward engagements would be won through discipline, training and comradeship, not through the individual prowess of the super-warriors Homer was to describe in the *Iliad*. In effect, the Age of Heroes was over, killed off by the progress of metallurgy.

Yet it continued to cast a long shadow. Throughout the long, illiterate centuries that followed the Dorian incursions, stories of heroic exploits in the Trojan War and elsewhere were kept alive and amplified by bards who would recite their ballads, with or without musical accompaniment, wherever there was an audience to pay them with the promise of a meal or a roof over their heads. These were the poets whose work Homer would one day inherit.

(see box, page 18), and that the epics were the work of many different bards.

The other fountainhead of Greek mythological knowledge was Homer's near-contemporary Hesiod. By occupation a farmer in the mainland province of Boeotia, it was he who, in his *Works and Days*, coined the idea of an Age of Heroes and gave it widespread currency. The poem sketches a pessimistic view of human history. In the earliest times, the poet claimed, there were men of gold who lived like gods and did not have to work for a living; they were followed by inferior generations, first of silver and then of bronze, who nonetheless were infinitely preferable to the race of iron among which the poet believed himself to be living. The pattern was one of progressive decline; yet Hesiod disturbed it by inserting an additional race – that of the heroes – between the ages of bronze and iron.

The reason why is easy enough to guess: he had to make allowance for the semi-legendary figures who had fought at Thebes and Troy. Evidently they were thought of in his day as having really existed, but were also held to have somehow been of greater stature than those who had come after them. Hesiod calls them righteous and noble, demigods who after death were transplanted by Zeus to the Isles of the Blessed, a distant paradise in the remote Western Ocean: "fortunate heroes for whom the abundant soil bears its honey-sweet fruits three times a year".

Homer and Hesiod between them fixed the image of the heroes that was to endure throughout the classical age and beyond. Their works were taught to all schoolchildren, and youngsters also heard them as bedtime tales; adults paid to hear rhapsodes – professional performers who recited the epics of Homer and other poets unaccompanied – or citharodes, who chanted the verses to the plucking of a lyre. There were other channels, too, by which the old stories were remembered. The religious festivals that sprang up around the renascent Greek world provided venues for passing on knowledge of the myths. Contests were held for reciters, and there were public lectures and addresses by travelling orators and scholars.

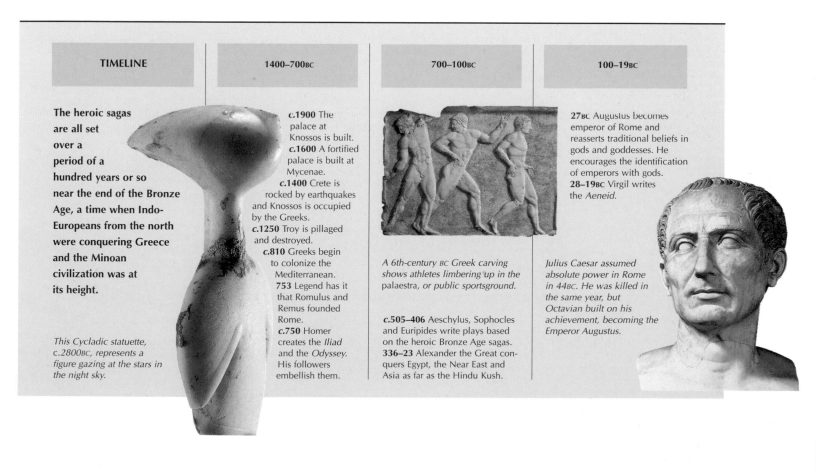

TIMELINE	1400–700BC	700–100BC	100–19BC

The heroic sagas are all set over a period of a hundred years or so near the end of the Bronze Age, a time when Indo-Europeans from the north were conquering Greece and the Minoan civilization was at its height.

This Cycladic statuette, c.2800BC, represents a figure gazing at the stars in the night sky.

*c.*1900 The palace at Knossos is built.
*c.*1600 A fortified palace is built at Mycenae.
*c.*1400 Crete is rocked by earthquakes and Knossos is occupied by the Greeks.
*c.*1250 Troy is pillaged and destroyed.
*c.*810 Greeks begin to colonize the Mediterranean.
753 Legend has it that Romulus and Remus founded Rome.
*c.*750 Homer creates the *Iliad* and the *Odyssey*. His followers embellish them.

A 6th-century BC Greek carving shows athletes limbering up in the palaestra, or public sportsground.

*c.*505–406 Aeschylus, Sophocles and Euripides write plays based on the heroic Bronze Age sagas.
336–23 Alexander the Great conquers Egypt, the Near East and Asia as far as the Hindu Kush.

27BC Augustus becomes emperor of Rome and reasserts traditional beliefs in gods and goddesses. He encourages the identification of emperors with gods.
28–19BC Virgil writes the *Aeneid*.

Julius Caesar assumed absolute power in Rome in 44BC. He was killed in the same year, but Octavian built on his achievement, becoming the Emperor Augustus.

An important new medium saw the light of day in the mid-sixth century, when dramas were first staged at the Festival of Dionysus in Athens. Much surviving knowledge of the hero myths now comes from the great Athenian playwrights of the following century: Aeschylus wrote of the murder of Agamemnon and of the Seven against Thebes; Sophocles of Antigone, Electra and King Oedipus; and Euripides's plays featured many mythological protagonists, including Alcestis, Heracles and Jason's sorceress wife Medea.

By that stage the city-state culture of the classical age was in its full flowering. The Greek world was divided into dozens, if not hundreds, of separate political entities. Some were ruled by single individuals, but many others followed the Athen-ian route of democracy by which all free males had the right to a say in the running of public affairs. Although the franchise did not extend to women or to the slave underclass, it nonetheless brought a larger section of the population into the processes of government than any political system the world has yet known.

At first sight, the democratic principle of shared civic rights might seem to have little in common with the heroic spirit, which emphasized the individual's quest for honour. In practice, though, the new democracies had little difficulty in adapting it to their own requirements. For the personal glory sought by a Heracles or an Achilles, they substituted the city's collective prestige. The path to distinction now lay in sacrificing personal

Singer of Heroes

Many scholars have questioned whether the powerful, well-constructed narratives of the Greek heroes attributed to Homer were the work of an individual poet.

The two great works ascribed to Homer, the *Iliad* and the *Odyssey*, are thought to have been written down sometime between 725 and 675BC, shortly after Greece relearned writing after four centuries of illiteracy. Both probably drew on a repertoire of ballads handed down orally by generations of reciters. Recognizing the importance of the traditional material, scholars in the eighteenth and nineteenth centuries questioned whether an

A Greek sculpture of *c.*150BC imagined what the *Iliad's* author might have looked like. This bust is a Roman copy (*c.*AD150) of the original.

individual poet named Homer had ever really existed. At best, they suggested, he might have been an editor drawing together material that originated centuries before. Many tried to deconstruct the epics into sections that, they claimed, had been written by individual poets. But no two experts could agree on just where those sections might begin or end.

More recently, academic opinion – citing the dramatic unity of the two works – has come back to the idea that each one was given its present shape by a single poet. What no one has ever questioned is the extraordinary force of the poems, which between them formed the basis for all subsequent Greek literature.

interests for the common good, and in demonstrating valour not for oneself but the community.

The new attitude embraced competitive sport, which assumed growing importance after the foundation of the Olympic Games, according to tradition in the year 776BC. Physical development was an important part of Greek education, and awareness of the ideal masculine physique was heightened by the fact that young men habitually exercised naked in the gymnasia that were a feature of all sizeable cities. At the games, successful competitors brought glory to the communities they represented. On their return home they received delirious public welcomes and were showered with civic honours. Before long, tradition was insisting that Heracles himself had staged the first games at Olympia and had instituted the custom of rewarding winners with a laurel crown.

War Heroes

The other main outlet for the heroic spirit was in war. The tactical revolution that had exalted the infantry at the expense of chariot-borne warriors also put a new stress on teamwork and discipline. The soldiers who made up a phalanx of infantry moved en masse and the men fought in close ranks, with each individual dependent on his neighbour's steadfastness for his own security.

The heroic outlook reached its apogee in the campaigns against the Persians who invaded Greece in 490BC and again nine years later. At the time the Persian Empire was the world's principal superpower, and little, disunited Greece must have seemed like an easy target. But for once a sense of common culture and nationhood drew the perpetually squabbling city-states together. At the same time the magnitude of the threat brought out a deep vein of patriotism and shared purpose that was to give the Greek people what they ever afterwards regarded as their finest hour.

If any one action can be said to sum up the spirit of the time, it was the defence of the pass of

In the era of the city-states, athletes competed out of civic pride. The winners were hymned in odes by great poets such as Pindar and were seen almost as reincarnations of the heroes of old.

Thermopylae, where the mountains of central Greece came down to within fifteen metres of the sea, in 480BC. For two days the combined Greek forces held this narrow passage against the invaders; then the Persians bribed a local farmer to show them a way through the hills, from which they would come out to the rear of the defenders. The Greeks learned that the enemy were coming and that they must inevitably be overwhelmed. They made the decision to withdraw, but knew they needed to leave a rearguard to hold back the Persians long enough for the rest to retire in safety.

The Spartan commander Leonidas volunteered for the task. He and his men guessed that the odds against them were insuperable and that none of them would come out alive – and so it turned out. From dawn the next morning, the 300 men took on the might of an invasion force 100,000 strong, attacking on two fronts. They fought the invaders with swords and daggers, and when their weapons were torn from them they continued desperately fighting with hands, feet and teeth until they fell. After many hours, the last of them was dead and the passage was clear; but the rest of the Greek army was safe and intact, and went on decisively to repel the invaders at the battles of Salamis and Plataea.

In such an atmosphere of exalted valour, it was hardly surprising that the heroes of old were frequently invoked. Orators called upon the spirit of Achilles and Heracles, and rumours spread that Theseus himself had been seen in full armour, fighting alongside the Athenian troops at the Battle of Marathon. The sense of steely resolve that suffused the land was summed up in the oath sworn by every Greek warrior before the final, decisive encounter at Plataea: "I shall fight to the death; I shall put freedom before life."

Such a high level of unity and purpose could not be sustained after the Persians were driven back to the Asian mainland. The history of Greece over the next 150 years was one of cultural triumph but of political decline, as the city-states that had come together to confront Xerxes were riven by factionalism and civil war.

The Last Hero

Yet Greece's heroic days were not over. A man who took his inspiration more directly than any other from the great figures of legend had still to make his mark, and in the year 336BC he acceded to the throne of a new power on the outer fringes of the Greek world. He was Alexander the Great, and he became King of Macedon after his father Philip was assassinated while putting together plans for a Greek invasion of Asia.

To the inhabitants of the Greek heartland, Macedonia – on the Aegean's northern shore – was a semi-barbarous place. Philip, however, had defeated the combined forces of Athens and Thebes and made himself master of the entire country. Alexander built on his father's success by first securing Macedonian control over Greece, then leading the army that Philip had built up across the Hellespont into Asia.

What followed was one of history's great adventure stories. The young ruler, just 22 years old when he launched the invasion, overwhelmed a Persian force at the Granicus river and went on over the next three years to make himself master of Asia Minor, Syria, the eastern Mediterranean seaboard and finally Egypt. Moving on to

In Greek infantry units the men fought side by side with heavy round shields linked for protection. Strong bonds of unity and comradeship were fostered. This Greek vase shows a fight to the death after the infantry units have broken up.

Mesopotamia, he again defeated the Persian emperor Darius and proceeded to mop up the remainder of his realm. Pursuing the fleeing ruler, Alexander led his men into today's Afghanistan; and even after Darius had been murdered by one of his own satraps, Alexander continued to press onward – through Uzbekistan and over the Hindu Kush mountains to the Indian sub-continent. There his men, after eight years of almost continuous travel and fighting, refused to go any further. So with great difficulty the army made its way back to Babylon, where Alexander died of a fever at the age of thirty-three.

Alexander's meteoric progress reflected the influence of the hero tales. Heracles was the purported founder of the royal house of Macedon to which Alexander belonged, and in the course of his career the young general deliberately emulated some of his legendary forefather's exploits. At Sidon in Lebanon, for instance, he was once nearly killed confronting a lion just as Heracles had done in his youth (see page 67). He was also depicted wearing the lionskin outfit of the great hero. Alexander was also greatly influenced by the works of Homer. As a boy he learned long passages of the *Iliad* by heart, and throughout his campaigns he reportedly carried the poem with him for bedtime reading. Before embarking on his assault on the Persians he took time to visit the ruins of Troy, where he laid a wreath on the mound believed to mark Achilles's grave. He took away an ancient shield that he subsequently always bore for luck into battle.

In his horsemanship, too, there was more than a hint of the heroic, recalling Bellerophon's exploits with the winged steed Pegasus. When he was barely in his teens, Alexander tamed the famous stallion Bucephalus when no one else could control it. Thereafter the horse would allow no other rider to climb onto its back, yet would kneel obediently to welcome Alexander into the saddle whenever he approached.

Even Alexander's weak points sometimes bore the hallmark of legend. His growing conviction of his own divinity probably owed as much to stories of Heracles's assumption to Mount Olympus (see page 77) as to oriental concepts of god-kings. And when in the course of a drunken

21

quarrel he killed one of his father's old retainers, a man who had once saved his own life, he was inconsolable until a priest convinced him that some god must have made him mad just as Hera had goaded Heracles into killing his own children (see page 68), so he could not be held responsible for his own action.

The Greeks' Wide Influence

The vast empire that Alexander had built up fragmented shortly after his death, and it was never to be reunited. Yet the tide of Greek culture that had swept across Asia and Egypt in his wake did not recede, and knowledge of the Greek hero myths spread with it to areas they had never before penetrated.

The myths had long since found their way across the Mediterranean to Italy, where Greeks had established colonies as early as the eighth century BC. There they were eventually assimilated by the inhabitants of the Latin-speaking town of Rome. That fact had little importance at the time, but the subsequent rise in the city's fortunes was to

The Roman emperor Augustus is honoured as a god (*centre, top*) while his successor Tiberius climbs from his war chariot (*left*) in this Roman carving.

make it highly significant. Within fifty years of Alexander's death the Romans were masters of the Italian peninsula. Defeat of Hannibal's Carthage seventy years later made them an international power, and after another century they had brought Greece itself under their sway. Thereafter they embarked on a course of expansion that won them an empire even Alexander might have envied, stretching from the Scottish border to Arabia, and from the Caspian Sea to Spain.

The Romans looked to Greek culture as a source of enlightenment, and provided an eager audience for hero legends that accorded well with their own native concepts of courage and honour. Soon Heracles had been Romanized as Hercules and Odysseus as Ulysses, and stories of Perseus and Jason were as familiar to Roman schoolchildren as they ever were to their Greek counterparts.

As Greek learning came to dominate intellectual life, it became fashionable to claim ancestry from the Greek heroes or to cite them as founders of Roman cities. Heracles himself had the city of Herculaneum named in his honour; it was to be destroyed along with Pompeii when Mount Vesuvius erupted in AD79. But by far the most influential of the foundation myths featured not a Greek hero but a Trojan. Aeneas appears in Homer's *Iliad* as the only member of the Trojan royal house to escape when Troy falls. The sea god Poseidon prophesies that Aeneas and his progeny will one day rule the surviving remnants of the Trojan people – a prediction that at some point became transferred to the Romans.

In time a legend grew up to the effect that Aeneas, after fleeing Troy, had found his way first to Carthage and then on to the future site of Rome, where he founded a city. On the basis of these disjointed tales the poet Virgil, writing shortly before the start of the Christian era, devised the last great epic of the classical world, the *Aeneid*, which remained uncompleted at his death in 19BC. It provided a heroic genealogy for Rome's founders and glorified Augustus, the Roman ruler.

Augustus initiated the imperial period of Rome's history; and by linking Rome's first emperor with a Homeric hero, Virgil brought the wheel of legend full circle. The legacy of the heroes had been soldered on to the Roman imperial dream, and from there on to the collective inheritance of the entire Western world.

Builder of Cities

In his eastward voyage of conquest, Alexander the Great created sixteen new cities named Alexandria. But the greatest by far was the one at the mouth of the Nile, which was to become the foremost metropolis of the classical world.

Founded in 332BC, Alexandria quickly rose to prominence, becoming capital of Egypt under the Ptolemaic dynasty within twenty years of Alexander's death. In the ensuing centuries it controlled much of the trade of the eastern Mediterranean and its population swelled to not far short of a million people.

Its cultural importance was, if anything, even greater. Its two celebrated libraries, one contained in the Museum, the other in a Temple of Zeus, were reputedly the largest in the ancient world, between them containing almost half a million different papyrus rolls. The university that developed around the Museum counted the mathematician Euclid and Aristarchus of Samothrace, the collator of the Homeric manuscripts, among its teachers.

In time Alexandria became a centre for the scholarly study of the old myths, and several encyclopaedic compilations were drawn up that helped preserve them into the modern age. It was there too that the association between mythology and astronomy was cemented, with the constellations being given the names of gods and heroes that they bear to this day. At the same time poets of the Alexandrian school sought inspiration in the old stories, often embellishing them with sentimental and romantic detail to suit the literary tastes of the Hellenistic world.

In his conquest of Asia and Egypt Alexander won enduring fame for Greece and for himself – in Egypt he was even revered as a god. This marble bust of the young general is a Roman copy of a 4th-century BC original.

QUESTS AND TRIALS

The tales of the heroes can be read together as one long story cycle that tells the history of the noble families of Bronze Age Greece – an ancient soap opera that includes love, war, jealousy and betrayal over half a dozen generations. Perseus, Bellerophon and Jason and his Argonauts were among the first wave of heroes; the combatants at Troy were the last.

The social world the heroes inhabit is a small one. They often appear in each other's stories: Heracles sails with the *Argo*; Odysseus fights at Troy. The same monsters – the Cyclopes, the Gorgons – plague them and the same women seduce or betray them. The sorceress Medea first marries Jason and then appears in a later tale as Theseus's stepmother. An ageing Theseus helps his friend to pursue Helen before her marriage to Menelaus.

But the physical world of the heroes encompassed the entire known world, from the pillars of Hercules – today's Rock of Gibraltar – to Colchis on the eastern shores of the Black Sea. For the audience of these sagas was a nation of travellers: Greek merchants traded the length and breadth of the Mediterranean and Black Seas, and Greek colonists founded great cities outside their homeland, from Sicily to Alexandria in Egypt.

If anything, the imaginative and emotional landscape inhabited by the heroes was vaster still. Bizarre creatures, fair princesses, strange omens and, of course, the great gods of Olympus all play their parts in the tales. Sometimes they simply explain natural phenomena: the winged horse Pegasus carries Zeus's lightning bolts; the home of the fire-breathing Chimera in Asia Minor was marked by flames of burning natural gas emerging from the ground. Sometimes they add colourful detail, as when Pegasus creates springs by stamping a hoof. But what makes the Greek sagas truly outstanding is their emotional depth and powerful characterization.

Usually the offspring of a mortal and a god, a Greek hero experienced human emotions on a divine scale – and he was never immune to anguish. In fact, despite their great exploits all the heroes except Heracles become lonely and bitter in old age and died tragically.

Left: **The goddess Hera's protection was vital for many of the heroes – and she was driven by jealousy to persecute others. This terracotta sculpture shows her at her most benign.**

Opposite: **The famous oracle at Delphi plays a major role in all the myths of the heroes. Again and again, the oracle is consulted and its commands and warnings set the ensuing drama in motion. Pictured left is the great temple.**

25

Perseus, Slayer of Medusa

Royal blood mixed with Olympian strength in the warrior Perseus. Born in Argos, he was the son of the Greek princess Danae and Zeus, the father of the gods. His remarkable destiny was predicted by the oracle at Delphi even before his birth.

Abas was king of the Argolid, the country around the city of Argos. On his death, he bequeathed his kingdom to his twin sons Proetus and Acrisius, instructing them to reign alternately. But the twins were bitter enemies – and when Proetus slept with Acrisius's daughter Danae, their quarrel grew more bitter still. Finally they agreed to divide the kingdom. Proetus took Tiryns and the coastal parts of the Argolid, while Acrisius took Argos itself.

Acrisius had no sons to inherit his part of the kingdom, and when he visited the oracle to seek advice he was told: "You will never have a son, but you will be succeeded by your daughter's son, who will kill you." Acrisius saw that he could escape this fate if he made sure that Danae had no children. Therefore he locked her away in an underground dungeon with doors made of bronze and set fierce dogs to guard the prison.

But the god Zeus fell in love with Danae and found a way to visit her. He transformed himself into a shower of gold that magically fell through the dungeon's ceiling and landed in Danae's lap. From this union, Danae bore a son named Perseus. Acrisius was convinced that the baby was the child described in the oracle's prophecy, who would depose and kill him, and he looked for a way to

Danae, holding her baby Perseus, rests on the island of Seriphos after being saved from certain drowning by the fisherman Dictys. This mural from Pompeii, dating from the 1st century AD, also depicts the wooden chest in which Danae and Perseus were launched on the sea. Perseus's father, the god Zeus, made sure that his son did not drown but came safely to land on Seriphos.

The Shifting Shapes of Zeus

Zeus, king of the gods and master of Olympus, seduced many mortal women, among them Perseus's mother, Danae, to whom he appeared as a shower of gold.

Zeus chose queens and princesses among mortal women and many heroes were the offspring of these liaisons. But the king of the gods did not generally allow mortals to see him in his divine glory, so he used a range of disguises. To Io, a princess of Argos, he appeared as a cloud. He disguised himself as a white bull to approach Europa. When he wanted to seduce Semele, he appeared to her as a mortal so as not to frighten the princess. But one day, prompted by Zeus's jealous wife Hera, Semele asked to see him in his glory. Dazzled by his Olympian magnificence, she burnt to ashes. Antiope, the Theban princess, was seduced by Zeus in the form of a satyr. But he used a still more subtle trick to make love to Alcmene,

the queen of Tiryns. He visited her as her husband and made three nights into one in order to extend his pleasure.

Zeus's seductions have been a favourite theme for artists. The 16th-century Venetian Titian produced several versions of Danae's ravishing.

be rid of both Danae and her son. He was afraid to slaughter them and so bring on himself the guilt of having spilled their blood, and instead he locked them in a wooden chest and cast them out to sea. He was sure they would be drowned.

After enduring many storms, the chest drifted towards the island of Seriphos. There, it was pulled ashore by a fisherman called Dictys, whose brother Polydectes was king of the island. Dictys forced the chest open, expecting to find treasure; but he was astonished to discover instead a mother and her baby boy. He took them to Polydectes, who agreed to give them shelter.

Perseus grew from a beautiful baby into a strong and handsome man, and his mother Danae, as she aged, also kept her good looks. King

Polydectes became infatuated with Danae and began to pester her with offers of marriage, but she resisted forcefully – and Perseus defended her. Polydectes decided that he might succeed with Danae if Perseus was not there, and so he devised a way of driving the young man away. Knowing that Perseus was too poor to have a horse of his own, Polydectes called the local nobles together and announced that he was planning to propose marriage to Princess Hippodameia and that he wished to take horses to her, as a gift. He asked each man to contribute a horse. Perseus, with his generous nature, fell into Polydectes's trap. He explained that he had no horse and no gold with which to buy one, but offered to bring Polydectes any other trophy he wanted.

27

Perseus presents the head of Medusa to Athene, in a detail from the Temple of Apollo in Rome. The goddess set the creature's head in her shield and used it to turn her enemies to stone.

Polydectes set Perseus what seemed an impossible task – to fetch him the head of the Gorgon Medusa. The Gorgons were three sisters, Medusa, Euryale, and Stheno, who lived at the western edge of the world and were the children of the sea creatures Phorcys and Ceto. Medusa had offended the goddess Athene, and had been made into a hideous, deadly monster. Her hair was a mass of writhing, hissing serpents and her glance was so terrible that anyone who gazed on her face was instantly turned to stone.

Perseus felt a cold fear at the hopelessness of his task. But the gods gave him special training and an armoury of magic weapons. First Athene herself came to his aid, glad of the chance to hurt Medusa still further. She took Perseus to the island of Samos and showed him a picture of all three Gorgons. She warned him not to try to kill Medusa's sisters Stheno and Euryale, because they were immortal, and reminded him not to look Medusa directly in the face, or he too would be turned to stone. "Take this polished shield, which shines like a mirror," she said. "Look only at Medusa's reflection as you kill her."

But Perseus needed more than cunning and a shield to overcome Medusa. From Hermes he received a sickle of magically strengthened iron to cut off Medusa's head. But even with these presents from the gods, Perseus was still too weak. Hermes and Athene advised him to ask for three magic objects from the nymphs of the dark and dangerous River Styx, which was the boundary between the Earth and the Underworld.

Perseus went to see the Graeae, three women who had been old since the day they were born, to ask directions to the Styx. The Graeae were sisters of the Gorgons and Perseus realized that trickery was the only way he could force them to tell him what he wanted to know.

The three old women had only one eye and one tooth between them. Whenever one of them wanted to look at something or to chew some food, she had to ask one of her sisters to pass the eye or tooth. Perseus crept up behind the women and snatched both the eye and the tooth. He then forced the Graeae to tell him what he should do to find the Stygian nymphs.

When he arrived at the river, the nymphs gave him a pair of winged sandals, a helmet to make him invisible and a satchel in which to carry the Gorgon's head after he had severed it. Perseus used the sandals to fly to the far west, where the Gorgons lived. The approach to their lair was littered with what looked at first like statues. But as he came nearer Perseus saw with horror that these were the remains of creatures that had been turned to stone by Medusa's glance.

The Gorgons were asleep. Perseus avoided Stheno and Euryale and manoeuvred the shield until it caught the reflection of the slumbering Medusa. Scarcely daring to breathe he inched towards her, taking care at every step not to rouse her or her sisters, until at last he stood with the magical sickle upraised. With Athene guiding his hand he sliced off Medusa's deadly head with one sweep. As he did so, he heard the sound of Athene's flute playing the "tune of many snakes' heads". Blood spurted from Medusa's neck. Perseus watched in astonishment as the armed warrior Chrysaor and the winged horse Pegasus leapt from her body. Then, without looking at Medusa's head, Perseus bundled it into the magic satchel and ran. Chrysaor and Pegasus did not chase him but the commotion woke Medusa's sisters who flew after him. But using his helmet to make himself invisible, Perseus escaped.

Donning his winged sandals, Perseus flew south to the lands of the giant Atlas, but he was not made welcome. To avenge this insult, he turned the giant to stone with the aid of Medusa's head. Atlas became a mountain for ever after, and the Greeks associated him with the Atlas range of peaks in Morocco, northern Africa. Perseus flew on. As he crossed the Libyan desert, some drops

A Hero's Bag of Tricks

For all their bravery and strength, the heroes of Greek myth were still in need of the gods' help. The gods often gave the hero a weapon or other object with magical properties, which enabled him to overcome the seemingly insuperable obstacles or unbeatable opponents that came his way.

The magical weapons that gave the hero special powers might be lent to him freely or they might have to be wrested from an unwilling owner. Finding the weapons often formed a preliminary search before the myth's main quest could begin.

Once acquired, the weapons enabled the hero to perform an activity – such as flying or cutting – that was a vital part of the main quest. Perseus, for example, used a magic sickle and shield to kill Medusa. Divine aids to action could also include spells, charms or animals such as Pegasus. Just as a bow and arrow extended a warrior's physical abilities, a magical weapon was an extension of the heroic qualities that a man already possessed. With the weapon the gods lent the hero a divine dimension. But when the hero misused it – as when Bellerophon used Pegasus in an attempt to fly to the peak of Mount Olympus (see page 35) – he was destroyed.

A detail from a 4th-century BC vase shows Perseus holding the magic sickle given to him by the god Hermes.

Still clasping Medusa's head, Perseus lays claim to Andromeda in a 1st-century AD fresco from Pompeii. The goddess Athene later made Perseus, Andromeda and Andromeda's parents, Cepheus and Cassiopeia, into constellations in the night sky.

of blood from Medusa's head fell on to the sand and turned into a writhing heap of poisonous snakes. From Libya he skirted the coasts of Egypt and Syria, heading back north towards Greece.

A Princess in Danger

Flying north along the Syrian coast, Perseus caught sight of a beautiful woman on the seashore. She was naked except for her jewellery and tied to a cliff with heavy iron chains. Nearby on the shore a richly dressed king and queen stood weeping. Perseus alighted and asked them: "What country have I reached and who is this beautiful maiden in such a fearful state?" Then the king, whose name was Cepheus, told him a terrible tale. His wife Cassiopeia had foolishly boasted that she and her daughter were more beautiful than the sea nymphs, the Nereids. This infuriated the sea god Poseidon, who sent a flood to Cepheus's kingdom,

Joppa. Not satisfied with the devastation caused by the flood, Poseidon then despatched a slavering sea-monster that devoured humans. Cepheus asked the oracle how he could appease the god. He was given an awful reply: he must sacrifice his own daughter, Andromeda, to the sea-monster.

Perseus was overwhelmed by the beauty of the frightened princess and without hesitation he replied: "King Cepheus, cease your weeping. I will rescue your daughter from this terrible fate. But you must promise that you will let me marry her and take her back home with me to Seriphos."

Cepheus and Cassiopeia were relieved that a hero had appeared to save their daughter. They agreed to Perseus's terms, but both secretly planned to go back on the deal once their daughter was safe. Cassiopeia had already agreed to marry Andromeda to a local prince named Agenor.

Unaware of their intentions, Perseus waited for the monster to appear. Soon a dreadful creature slithered across the shore towards Andromeda. Unaware that a hero had come to rescue her, she screamed and struggled. Then Perseus flew overhead, casting a shadow on the surface of the water that momentarily distracted the monster. Instantly Perseus swooped down and beheaded it with his sickle. He also took the opportunity to dispose of the Medusa's head, laying it face down on the sea bed, where it turned the seaweed into coral.

The royal party on the shore cheered rapturously and began to celebrate Perseus's victory. Andromeda insisted on being married to Perseus at once, but this was not what her parents had planned. They agreed to go through with the ceremony, but secretly summoned Agenor, who arrived with a party of armed supporters demanding Andromeda as his own bride. Perseus fought Agenor and his followers for Andromeda, but he was outnumbered and was forced to retrieve the Gorgon's head from the seabed. Then holding it triumphantly up before him, he turned the warriors, as well as Andromeda's parents, to stone.

When Perseus returned with Andromeda to Seriphos, he found that his mother Danae and the fisherman Dictys had fled to a temple for refuge from Polydectes, who, during Perseus's absence, had continued to pester Danae to marry him. Perseus went to the palace, where the king was holding a riotous feast. While the drinkers hurled insults at him, Perseus stood firm in their midst and declared: "Polydectes, you thought you would never see me again. But here I am. And I have brought you the wedding present you asked for." Polydectes mocked him, refusing to believe that Perseus had defeated the terrible Medusa. Then Perseus, turning his face away for safety, pulled Medusa's head from the pouch and held it up. Instantly, Polydectes and the assembled feasters were turned to stone.

Perseus returned his magic objects to Hermes and Athene. Hermes delivered the wallet, helmet and sandals to the Stygian nymphs. Perseus installed Dictys as the king of Seriphos and then set out for Argos, the birthplace that he had not seen since infancy, in order to claim his rightful throne from Acrisius. Acrisius heard that Perseus was on his way. He still lived in fear of the oracle's prophecy and fled to Larissa in Thessaly.

But he could not escape his destiny. The old king of Larissa died and Perseus was invited to join the funeral games being staged by Teutamides, the new king, in honour of his father. During the games, Perseus took part in a discus competition. When he stepped forward to make his throw, the gods sent a gust of wind that carried the discus off course. It struck Acrisius, killing him instantly. In this way the oracle was fulfilled and Acrisius was indeed slain by the son of his daughter Danae.

The discus became a lethal weapon when Perseus accidentally killed his grandfather in an athletic contest. In some versions of the myth the accident took place at the funeral games of Polydectes of Seriphos rather than at those of the king of Larissa.

Tamer of the Winged Horse

A handsome prince of Corinth, Bellerophon was a son of the sea god Poseidon according to some authors. Forced to flee the Corinthian court, he was dogged by ill fortune on his travels, and his good looks and modesty only caused him further trouble.

Bellerophon was a fearless young man who was drawn into a violent quarrel in which he killed his brother and another man. He escaped from his home in Corinth to the court of King Proetus of Tiryns, where he approached the king as a suppliant, asking humbly for shelter. The unexplained arrival of a good-looking stranger caused quite a stir, and Proetus's wife Anteia fell in love with Bellerophon. But when she tried to persuade him to take her to bed the young man refused. Naturally, Anteia was furious and she accused him, in front of her husband, of having tried to seduce her.

Proetus was in an awkward position. Custom dictated that he should kill anyone who made advances on his wife, but Bellerophon had come to him as a suppliant and suppliants were protected by Zeus. Instead of killing him, Proetus sent Bellerophon to Lycia in Asia Minor, carrying a letter to Proetus's father-in-law, Iobates, the Lycian king. The letter said that Bellerophon had tried to seduce Anteia – Iobates's daughter – and asked Iobates to put the bearer to death. But according to custom, Iobates could not kill a guest, so he devised an ordeal that he was sure Bellerophon would not survive.

The Lycian king asked him to track down and destroy the Chimera, a fire-breathing female monster with a lion's body and head, a second goat's head protruding from her back and a snake in place of a tail. The Chimera was the daughter of

Eichidne, a nymph with a snakelike lower body, and the monster Typhon. She had been terrorizing Iobates's kingdom for a long time.

Bellerophon had no idea how to go about this fearsome task, so he decided to consult the seer Polyeidus, who told him of a white, winged horse named Pegasus. Wherever this steed stamped the ground with his hoof, a spring of fresh water rose. If Bellerophon could find Pegasus by one of these springs, and manage to harness and ride him, he would then be able to complete his task.

This was easier said than done, for Pegasus was a wild, free animal, and although Bellerophon was strong, he knew that he would never be able to control the winged horse on his own. Fortunately, Athene came to the hero's aid, giving him a golden bridle and instructing him to sacrifice a white bull to her uncle Poseidon, god of the sea and tamer of horses. After making the sacrifice, Bellerophon found he was able to tame Pegasus with the bridle.

The magic horse swiftly brought Bellerophon to where the Chimera was rampaging across the countryside. Clinging to Pegasus's muscular back, Bellerophon soared over the Chimera's head and fired volley after volley of arrows into the monster's body. But, despite this attack, the Chimera would not die, and Bellerophon realized that the only way to destroy the monster was to turn her own powers against her. Fixing a lump of lead to the tip of a spear, he flew directly at her

Bellerophon rides the winged horse Pegasus, on a clay fragment from Thasos, dated c.540–500BC.

The Language of Animals

Not long after Proetus sent Bellerophon to Lycia, a young healer called Melampus came to his kingdom. Melampus was a man of rare gifts who could understand the language of animals.

Melampus had made his reputation as a healer by curing King Phylacus's son Iphiclus of impotence. When Phylacus asked him to heal his son, Melampus sacrificed two bulls to Apollo, and as two vultures swooped to feed off the remains, he overheard their conversation. They recalled how when Iphiclus was still a boy they had seen Phylacus castrating rams at this spot. The king came towards the boy with his bloody knife and Iphiclus took fright thinking he, too, was to be castrated.

Phylacus stuck the knife into a nearby tree while he comforted his son, but the fright had made the boy impotent. The vultures said that Iphiclus could be cured if the knife was pulled out of the tree and the ram's blood was scraped off it and given to Iphiclus in a drink. Melampus did what they suggested and cured Iphiclus.

Meanwhile, Proetus had troubles of his own: his three daughters had taken to roaming the mountainside assaulting travellers. Worse still, the rest of the Argive women joined them, so Proetus's kingdom was in a shambles. Melampus told Proetus to sacrifice twenty red oxen to the gods. With the help of Artemis and Helios, he herded the women down the mountainside and then purified them in a holy well. But the daughters of Proetus hid in a cave by the River Styx. Eventually, Melampus found them and purified them too. He married the one called Lysippe and when Proetus died, inherited his kingdom.

head, but just before her fiery breath incinerated him, he thrust the spear into her open jaws. The fire melted the lead, which flowed down her gullet and burned up her innards.

The King's Fury

With the Chimera dead, Bellerophon returned triumphantly to the capital city. But Iobates was not at all grateful and sent Bellerophon on another quest – this time against the Solymians and the Amazons, who had been attacking Lycia. Once more Bellerophon defeated his enemies, on this occasion by flying above the armies on Pegasus's back and dropping rocks onto them. On the way back to Iobates he met a band of pirates who had also been harassing Lycia and defeated them too. Hearing of his success, the unforgiving Iobates sent palace guards to attack Bellerophon.

When he ran into the guards' ambush, Bellerophon finally realized that Iobates was trying to kill him. He dismounted from his winged steed, sending a prayer for help to Poseidon, who unleashed a tidal wave that followed Bellerophon

as he walked across the Xanthian plain. The king and his people were terrified to see Bellerophon advancing on their city with a wall of water behind him. Iobates sent messengers who begged Bellerophon to retire, but he was so angry that he would not take any notice. In desperation, the

Fire-breathing She-Monster

The creature that Bellerophon was sent to kill, the Chimera, was one of many female monsters who populated the mythological world of the Greeks.

The hybrid monsters of Greek mythology included snake-haired Medusa, the Sphinx – a winged lion with a woman's head – and the Harpies and the Sirens – both half woman, half bird. Some scholars have suggested that the predominance of female monsters suggests that the heroic sagas of the Greeks were metaphors for the conquest of the ancient Earth Mother

religion by the cult of the sky god Zeus. The ancient goddesses were demonized by followers of the new religion.

The Chimera – with the head of a lion, the tail of a snake or dragon and the head of a nanny goat placed in the middle of its back – is thought to have originated in the Near East. The civilizations of the Fertile

The wounded Chimera roars in pain. This beautiful Etruscan bronze was made between 380 and 360BC.

women of the city lifted their skirts and ran towards him – possibly to shame him but perhaps also as a signal that he could have any sexual reward he chose if he would only retreat. But Bellerophon turned and fled. As he ran, the wave retreated too so the city was reprieved.

Iobates was struck by Bellerophon's modesty and began to have his doubts about the letter that had come from Tiryns. He showed Bellerophon this letter and asked him to tell his side of the story. The hero was shocked to learn that he had been sent to Lycia to meet his death. Iobates begged his forgiveness, then offered Bellerophon the hand of the princess Philonoe in marriage and said he would make him heir to the Lycian throne.

Bellerophon's future looked bright, but just at the moment when he seemed to have escaped his ill fortune he provoked the gods to punish him. He was so excited by his ability to fly on Pegasus that he set off on the horse's back to travel to the gods' home on the summit of Mount Olympus. Zeus was furious and sent a mosquito to bite Pegasus under the tail. The horse reared, flinging Bellerophon to earth. He fell into a thornbush and his royal finery was torn to shreds.

Bellerophon spent the last days of his life wandering the Earth lame and blind, and avoiding other humans. As for Pegasus, he continued the journey to Olympus without his rider, and it was said that Zeus used him to carry thunderbolts.

Crescent had developed a whole bestiary of magical animals at least 1,000 years before Greek civilization began to flourish.

Although the Chimera is a remarkable and unusual creature, very little is actually recorded about her. The poet and mythographer Robert Graves suggested that the parts of her body represented the seasons of the agricultural year. Other scholars have suggested that her fire-breathing nature was a mythical explanation of the volcanic geisers found in southern Anatolia, where the tale of Bellerophon is set.

Since ancient times, the name "Chimera" has shifted in meaning and has come to be used more generally to denote any fantastic idea or grotesque, imaginary beast. The word has also been adapted by architects: *chimère* is a term that is used rather loosely to describe any mythical or exotic creature that has been added as a decorative feature to buildings.

Jason and the Argonauts

Jason was prepared by his upbringing for the trials of a hero. Born a prince of Iolcus, he was exiled from the royal palace after his uncle Pelias seized the throne, and was raised in a mountain wilderness by the centaur Chiron with a glittering array of other future heroes including Achilles and Aeneas. After schooling him in the medical arts, Chiron gave the prince the name of Jason, meaning "Healer".

As a young man Jason set out from Mount Pelion, where he had been raised, for the court of the usurper King Pelias in Iolcus. He intended to claim his father's throne as his rightful inheritance. On his way to the city he reached a river bank, where he helped an old woman who had asked him to carry her across. This old woman was the goddess Hera in disguise; she carried a hatred for Pelias in her heart since he had failed to honour her, and because Jason helped her she vowed to protect

him until the day of Pelias's death. As Jason carried Hera across the stream one of his sandals was washed away in the river. With one bare foot he walked on to Iolcus.

When Pelias's courtiers saw him they rushed to find their master. He had instructed them to watch for a man with one bare foot because the Delphic oracle had told him that a man arriving from the mountains wearing only one sandal would cause his death.

Jason stood tall in the public square. He was carrying two spears and had a leopard-skin flung around his shoulders against the driving rain; he had not cut his hair, and his locks flowed and curled down his back. When Pelias arrived there, he eyed the awe-struck citizens gathered around the young man and listened as they whispered to one another: "Can this be Apollo, or one of the great heroes of old?" Then the king saw that his servants had been right: the stranger was missing one sandal. Hiding his fear, Pelias asked Jason: "What country are you from, stranger, and who are your ancestors?"

Jason replied: "I am King Aeson's son and I was reared in the cave of Chiron the centaur, who taught me the healing arts and gave me the name Jason. After twenty years of a blameless life I have come to claim the throne that is rightfully mine." He went to the palace, where his aged, downcast father recognized him and wept. Jason's brothers also came to the palace and for five days they celebrated their reunion with feasting.

But on the sixth day they turned to business. Jason affirmed his claim to the throne, and they all agreed to help him. They strode fearlessly in to deliver their ultimatum to Pelias. But Jason was anxious to avoid a civil war, and so spoke without aggression. He told Pelias that because they were relations, they should not fight over the inheritance; he offered to allow Pelias to keep the land, cattle and sheep that belonged to the king of Iolcus if he returned the sceptre and the throne.

Pelias made a cunning reply. He recalled the history of Jason's cousins Phrixus and Helle, who had fled Greece to avoid being sacrificed by their stepmother. They escaped by flying on the back of a golden ram, sent by Hermes, to the distant land of Colchis at the eastern end of the Black Sea in modern Georgia. On the way Helle fell off into the sea – giving her name to the Hellespont, the

The gathering of the Argonauts was the largest assembly of heroes to take place in Greek legend until the Trojan War. This red-figure vase shows them before setting out.

narrow straits connecting the Aegean and the Sea of Marmara – but Phrixus arrived safely and to thank the gods he sacrificed the ram and hung its fleece from a tree. There it remained, guarded by a dragon. But when Phrixus died in Colchis he was not given a proper burial and his unquiet ghost continued to trouble his relatives. Pelias claimed that the only way to satisfy Phrixus was for a hero to travel to Colchis to bring back Phrixus's remains and the fabled golden fleece. He swore to give up the throne if Jason accepted this task.

The two men concluded their agreement and Jason sent out messengers to invite the finest young men to seek a hero's fate, even if it should lead to death. The volunteers were many, including Zeus's son Heracles, the strongest man in the world, and Orpheus the musician, son of Apollo.

The Greeks believed Delphi to be the centre of the Earth. It was the centre of the cult of Apollo; and prophecies of the oracle from Apollo's Temple revealed the destinies of heroes.

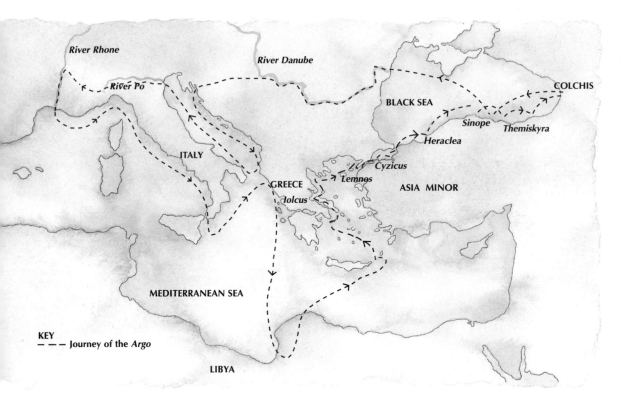

The tale of Jason and the Argonauts was retold many times and different authors plotted different routes. The one shown here is from the *Argonautica*, written by Apollonius of Rhodes in the 3rd century BC.

Boreas the North Wind sent his winged sons Zetes and Calais. Echion, Hermes's son, and Acastus, Pelias's son, also enrolled for the voyage.

The heroes built a ship, the *Argo*, of the finest wood. Jason's protectress, Athene, provided a bough from the sacred whispering oak tree at the oracle at Dodona, and this gave the ship itself the ability to speak. When the crew had all gathered on the beach at Pagasae, Jason took a golden bowl and made a prayer to Zeus for favourable winds and a safe homecoming. Zeus responded immediately with thunder and lightning, and the ship set sail. There were fifty-six "Argonauts" on board. While Tiphys steered the vessel, Orpheus made music to soothe the waves and mark time for the other men, who rowed in pairs.

The Voyage to Colchis

The Argonauts first came to land on the island of Lemnos, where during the previous year the men had argued with their wives and abandoned them for Thracian girls captured on raids. In revenge the

women slaughtered the men. The Lemnian women at first took the Argonauts for enemy raiders and greeted them in war formation, but they soon softened and took advantage of these handsome warriors to breed a new generation. The Argonauts might have remained indefinitely, if Heracles – who was guarding the ship – had not come striding in to remind them of their urgent mission.

The Argonauts' next port of call was Cape Arcton in the Sea of Marmara. Here they were given a warm welcome by King Cyzicus and invited to his wedding. But when they tried to sail away, a storm drove them back to shore on a dark night. In the darkness Cyzicus and his men mistook them for pirates and a battle followed in which Jason killed Cyzicus by mistake. The Argonauts took part in funeral games to honour the dead king. But Cleite, Cyzicus's bride, hanged herself in despair. The *Argo* sailed on to the island of Chios. Heracles's lover Hylas went to fetch water from a spring but was dragged under by a water-nymph who fell in love with his beauty and drowned him. The frantic Heracles, not knowing

The Calydonian Boar Hunt

Some authors say that the fearless hunter Meleager was one of the faithful band that sailed with Jason to Colchis on board the **Argo.** *If so he must have returned safely from the journey, for his destiny was played out in his homeland of Calydon, where his father Oineus was king.*

When Meleager was a baby, the Fates told his mother Althaea that her son's life would last only as long as a log then burning in the fire was unconsumed. She snatched it up, doused the flames and hid it. Meleager's father Oineus each year made a sacrifice to all the twelve Olympian gods, and his kingdom prospered with their favour. But one year he accidentally omitted the name of Artemis. In revenge, the goddess sent a gigantic boar that ravaged the country, killing cattle and farmers.

Oineus sent out a call for help, promising the tusks and skin of the boar to whoever killed it. Many renowned heroes assembled from all over Greece to hunt the beast under the leadership of Meleager. Some say Jason and Theseus were among them. There also came Atalanta, a girl who had been abandoned as a baby, suckled by a bear and raised by mountain hunters. She was a superb huntress and the fastest runner in the world.

But Artemis was using Atalanta as a tool to ruin Oineus.

Meleager fell in love with her and while the other hunters complained that a woman would bring them bad luck, he supported her participation and showed her unfair favour.

The expedition set out full of bad feeling. Once out in the forest, the hunters spread out and several were killed in a

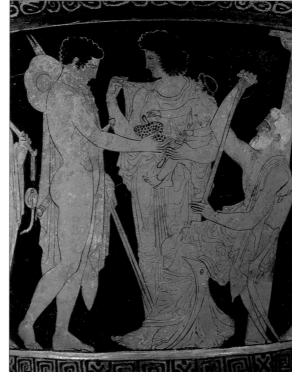

According to some versions of the story Meleager and Atalanta had a son, Parthenopaeus; this 5th-century BC vase shows him in his mother's arms.

series of horrible mishaps. Hylaeus and Rhaecus, two centaurs that were part of the group, tried to rape Atalanta and were shot by her, while the hunter Ancaeus was castrated and disembowelled by the boar's massive tusks. Atalanta was the first to injure the boar but it was Meleager who finally killed it. He presented its hide to Atalanta, but this act of generosity was too much for some of the other hunters. Toxeus and Plexippus, two of his mother's brothers, disputed Meleager's decision and in a rage he killed them both.

Meleager's mother watched the bodies of her brothers being carried back from the forest and cursed her son. She took the half-burned log from the chest in which she had hidden it and thrust it at once deep into the fire. Immediately Meleager died – according to some versions, as he fought his surviving uncles who had declared war on Calydon. His sisters shrieked as they mourned for him and Artemis turned them into guinea fowl. Althaea later hanged herself in remorse.

The Argonauts and King Aeetes of Colchis watch, awe-struck, as Jason tames one of the fire-breathing bulls that Aeetes has told the hero he must use to plough a field. The scene, carved on a stone coffin, also shows Eros, the boy-god of love, with his bow *(centre left)*. Eros was sent by his mother Aphrodite to make Aeetes's daughter Medea fall passionately in love with Jason. As well as giving Jason a potion that protected him from the bulls, Medea persuaded the hero to pray for help to Hecate, the goddess of witches.

where Hylas had gone, rushed off to look for his friend and never came back to the ship.

Once through the Hellespont into the Black Sea, the *Argo* stopped at the land of the Bebrycans, whose king was a keen boxer. The Argonaut Polydeuces killed him in a match. Further along the coast, they came upon blind King Phineus, who had enraged Zeus because in using his prophetic powers he had revealed some of the god's secrets. So Zeus sent the Harpies, monstrous flying women, to torment Phineus; every time he tried to eat, they snatched his food away. The winged Argonauts Zetes and Calais flew at the Harpies, chasing them back to the Aegean.

The Argonauts knew that to reach Colchis they had to pass through the Symplegades, a pair of floating rocks that would smash together to crush any ship that tried to pass between them. Phineus advised the Argonauts to send a dove ahead of the ship. If it got through, he said, they must row as hard as they could between the rocks while they were moving away from each other after banging together. Following his directions, they made it past the rocks, which from that day forward stopped moving. Finally, after passing the land of the Amazons and of the iron-smelting Chalybes, the Argonauts entered the mouth of the River Phasis in the land of Colchis.

Trials to Win the Golden Fleece

Jason and a party of the Argonauts went to the palace of Aeetes, king of Colchis and son of Helios the sun god. The first person to see them was Aeetes's daughter Medea, who under a spell imposed by the goddess Aphrodite fell in love with Jason in an instant. Aeetes himself was alarmed by the Argonauts' arrival because he thought that they had come to depose him, but he hid his hatred of them. When Jason asked to be allowed to take the golden fleece, Aeetes pretended to agree to the request, but said the hero must first pass a test – Jason would have to plough a field using two bulls given to him by Aeetes, and then sow seed also provided by the king.

Medea's heart was ablaze with love for Jason, and secretly she revealed to him the hidden dangers in her father's plans. The bulls, she said, had brazen hooves and breathed fire. The seeds were teeth of the dragon that Cadmus, founder of Thebes, had killed. She recalled how when Cadmus had sowed some of the teeth on Athene's instructions, armed warriors had sprouted from the ground; he had thrown a stone amongst them that made them fight and kill one another. Medea gave Jason an ointment to protect him from the bulls and suggested he use a stone against the warriors.

When it was time for the ordeal, Aeetes presented Jason with a plough of magically hardened metal and the fearsome oxen. The king had special powers over the animals and he himself ploughed the first furrow. Then he challenged the captain of the *Argo* to complete the ploughing.

Jason threw off his saffron-coloured robe and, trusting to the gods, seized the handle of the plough. The oxen kicked him with their hooves and scorched him with their breath, but Medea's ointment protected his skin. Aeetes cried out in astonishment as Jason forced the animals to submit to his will. As Jason ploughed, huge clods of earth split off with a terrible rasping noise. He scattered the dragon's teeth into the furrows as he went, casting wary glances behind him in case they sprouted too quickly. But all went well, and it was not until he finished ploughing that he saw the first armed men rising out of the soil, bristling with swords and their armour glinting in the sunlight. Remembering Medea's advice, Jason flung a boulder into their midst and the soldiers, suspecting

each other of throwing the stone, began a fight to the death amongst themselves. Jason ran between the furrows with his sword and cut down the remaining soldiers where they sprouted.

Aeetes retreated bitterly to his palace and sat up all night wondering how to destroy this troublesome stranger once and for all. Medea too felt distress – she was convinced that her love for Jason had already been found out. She crept to the Argonauts' camp fire and begged them to hurry on to the dragon's grove before Aeetes caught up with them. "I shall charm the dragon to sleep," she said to Jason, "but may the gods remember your promise to marry me when I am far from my home with nobody to protect me." Pushing aside the undergrowth, they came upon the remains of the altar on which Phrixus had sacrificed the golden ram. Nearby lay the dragon, gazing at them menacingly. Medea began to sing to it and sprinkled sleep potions on its eyes. As the dragon relaxed, Jason carefully lifted the golden fleece from where it hung on a massive oak tree.

41

It was already daylight, and the Argonauts set out to sea without delay. No sooner had they pulled away from land, than Aeetes appeared on the shore with a huge army. Calling on Zeus to witness how he had been wronged, Aeetes set out in pursuit. But Hera sped the Argonauts onwards in her desire to bring Medea to Greece and there to use her as an instrument of revenge on Pelias.

In some versions, Medea brought her baby brother Aspyrtos with her on the return voyage. As her father's ship was drawing dangerously close, she cut the child into pieces which she scattered on the surface of the sea behind the ship. Her father was forced to stop to collect the remains so

he could give his son a decent funeral, and this gave the *Argo* the chance to evade pursuit.

The Argonauts went through many further trials on their return journey to Greece, including being chased around the island of Crete by the giant Talos. But finally one autumn evening, the ship drew in at the beach of Pagasae from which the Argonauts had set out so many adventures ago.

Talos, a bronze giant who attacked the Argonauts when they tried to land on Crete, falls under Medea's spell in this detail from a painted Greek vase of *c*.400BC. Medea gave Talos a sleeping draught; as he slumbered she pulled from his ankle a bronze nail that held in his lifeblood, and he bled to death.

Sisters of Night

Medea and her aunt Circe play a role in several of the heroes' stories. With their magical powers, these sorceresses made even the greatest warriors afraid. The deity who helped them was the mysterious goddess of the darkling moon, Hecate.

In Greek mythology the witch appears in several guises, but she is always a powerful and resourceful magician. Sometimes she is a cunning young temptress, motivated by passion to commit her crimes, and sometimes a wise crone who has a benign aspect as well as a propensity for vengeful acts.

The best known of all witches, unifying the domains of death and magic, is Hecate. The oldest of Greek goddesses, she may have had her origins in the Egyptian deity Hequit (or Heket) who was the goddess of midwives. Hecate was an Earth goddess associated with the realm of the dead. As a scion of the dark moon, she ruled over the deceased and the world of spirits who inhabited the night.

She is not mentioned in the works of Homer, although Hesiod describes her at length in his *Theogony*. He identifies her as the daughter of Coeus and Phoebe, but her parentage remains uncertain and it has been said that Zeus was her father. Demeter has also been named as her mother; both goddesses are associated with the ground and fertility.

Witches often performed rituals at crossroads, which Hecate was believed to frequent, for they were symbolic of the place where the Earth met the shadowy Underworld.

Circe, daughter of Helios the sun god and Perse, an Oceanid, was a beautiful woman, skilled in the magic arts, but doomed to an unhappy love life. She transformed her enemies into animals. Provoked by her experience of unrequited love, she took revenge on a character called Picus whom she turned into a woodpecker. Similarly, when the sea god Glaucus asked her for an aphrodisiacal potion to attract Scylla, Circe fell in love with him herself and transformed her opponent into a horrible monster, condemned to

The ancient goddess Hecate was often depicted as triple-faced. She carried a torch to light up the shadowy regions that she ruled and was followed by a pack of hell hounds.

guard the Straits of Messina. Homer describes Circe's island home as constantly circled by wild beasts, all victims of the witch's sorcery.

It was to Circe that Jason and Medea went for purification after the murder of Aspyrtos. Like her aunt, Medea was both passionate and scheming. Her name actually means "cunning" or "knowing". The myths tell that both she and her father were devotees of Hecate.

Medea's Revenge

Jason was bound to Medea by the solemn oath he had sworn on the beach at Colchis before she helped him to win the golden fleece. He knew that their destinies were linked and that as a witch she had a vast array of supernatural powers at her disposal.

On the evening that they returned to Iolcus with the fleece, the news that greeted the Argonauts was terrible. A lone boatman reported that Aeson and Polymele, Jason's parents, had been murdered by Pelias. Making the boatman promise to tell no one of the *Argo's* arrival, the men sat down to plot a soldier's revenge. But Medea promised them that she could single-handedly do away with Pelias, using her witch's skills.

She instructed them to conceal the boat and wait in hiding. They were to watch for a blazing torch on the roof of the palace in Iolcus, which would be a sign to attack the city. Then she cast a spell that transformed her into a wrinkled crone. She dressed her twelve maidservants in strange costumes and led them in procession towards Iolcus, carrying a statue of the goddess Artemis. When they reached the gates, she called out to the sentries: "The goddess Artemis has come to you from the foggy lands of the far north, riding in a chariot pulled by flying serpents. Let her in, so that she may bring good fortune to your city!" The sentries willingly let

them in and the women raced through the streets, shrieking and tearing their hair. Their behaviour roused the popula-tion of Iolcus to a frenzy of religious fervour.

Medea made her way to Pelias's chambers and told him that his son Acastus had died with the other Argonauts in a shipwreck off Libya. Then she said that the goddess Artemis had decided to restore him to youth so that he could beget another son to replace Acastus. As a demonstration, she undid the spell that had made her appear old and stood before him in all her radiant beauty. To convince him still further, she cut up an old ram and boiled it in a cauldron of mag-ical herbs, pulling out a young lamb that she had hidden. In one version of the myth, Medea also used this boiling treatment to bring Jason's father Aeson back to life and to make him young again.

The dramatist Euripides's interpretation of Medea's story fired the imagination of the ancient world and her infanticide was a popular theme. This fresco from Pompeii shows her contemplating the murder of her children.

King Pelias willingly consented to be dismembered and cooked if it meant recovering his youth. So Medea charmed him to sleep and instructed his daughters to cut him up – just as she had cut up the ram – and boil the pieces. But unlike the ram, the king failed to benefit from the treatment and instead died an agonizing death. To add insult to injury, while the cauldron was cooking, Medea led his daughters up to the palace roof and persuaded them to perform a rite to the moon with waving torches. The waiting Argonauts saw the signal and rushed into the city, taking it without resistance. But Jason would not accept the throne of Iolcus and passed it to Acastus, who had sailed with him on the *Argo* – perhaps fearing that Acastus, who was Pelias's son, would avenge his father's death. Jason and Medea went into exile, and after much wandering they settled in Corinth. Medea, through her father's side, was entitled to the rulership of Corinth, so when the throne fell vacant, she claimed it for Jason.

Medea, driven mad by rage at Jason's betrayal, puts one of their sons to the sword, in a Greek vase painting of *c.*320BC. In some versions of the myth her sons were killed by Corinthians.

Jason Betrays his Wife

Jason and Medea could not live happily together. Jason was unable to forget his wife's long record of murder and sorcery, and when the Theban king, Creon, offered him the hand of the princess Glauce in marriage, he agreed and told Medea that he intended to divorce her. She was furious. Angrily, she reminded Jason of the solemn oath to her that he had made in Colchis, and pointed out that he had relied on her help to win both the golden fleece and the throne of Corinth.

When Jason refused to change his mind she pretended to go along with his plan, but plotted revenge. She sent Glauce a wedding gift of a gold crown and a white robe that were bewitched. When the unsuspecting princess put on the robe she was seized by a consuming fire that ate searingly into her flesh and then spread through the crowd of wedding guests, killing every one of them except for Jason himself.

At this point, some say, the god Zeus was impressed with Medea's courage and fell in love with her, but she rejected him. Hera, his wife, was so pleased by this that she promised to make Medea's children immortal if the queen left them in her temple. Medea did so, escaping from Corinth with the help of her grandfather, Helios the sun god, who lent her his chariot. She fled to Athens, where King Aegeus offered her sanctuary. Medea was still an attractive woman and Aegeus later married her (see page 52).

But the angry population broke into Hera's temple and killed the children. In later years, the Corinthians were so ashamed of their behaviour that they bribed the playwright Euripides with fifteen talents of silver to write a play in which Medea murders her own children.

As for Jason, his end was pathetic and inglorious. In breaking his oath of fidelity to Medea he had broken his faith with the gods in whose name he had sworn. Some ancient authors claim that he died in Corinth, either by his own hand or murdered by the vengeful Medea. Others say that he wandered from city to city as a beggar, and as an old man sat down sorrowfully under the hulk of the *Argo* where it had been beached at Corinth. The prow, which had rotted away through years of neglect, fell off the ship and killed him.

MAGICAL BEASTS

One ordeal most heroes had to face at some point in their careers was a battle with a monster – typically a hybrid creature made up of parts of two or more different species. Such beasts were familiar in Babylonian and Egyptian mythology, which may have provided the inspiration for Greek exemplars like the Chimera and the Sphinx. What is certain is that by overcoming these preternatural adversaries the victors confirmed their more-than-mortal status more convincingly than they could ever have done by merely vanquishing conventional opponents.

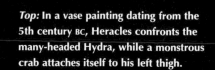

Top: In a vase painting dating from the 5th century BC, Heracles confronts the many-headed Hydra, while a monstrous crab attaches itself to his left thigh.

Above: Mounted on a terracotta Pegasus, Bellerophon stabs the fearsome Chimera, which combined a lion's head with a goat's body and a snakelike tail.

Above: His last labour over, Heracles presents Cerberus, the three-headed hound of Hades, to his tormentor Eurystheus, who cowers in a jar.

Right: Provided with a sword and a ball of twine by his lover Ariadne, Theseus spears the Minotaur, half-man and half-bull, in a painting decorating a 6th-century BC amphora, now in the British Museum.

WHEN MEN WERE GIANTS

Theseus, Oedipus and Heracles are heroes who have stood the test of time. More than three millennia after their lifetime – for the myths make them contemporaries – each is still a familiar name through much of the western world. The continuing popularity of their legends indicates that some element, whether in the heroes' characters or the stories about them, has given them an exceptional staying power.

There is a common pattern underlying the lives of all three heroes. All are of royal or divine birth, and all give evidence of abnormal strength or courage even as children. Each faces obstacles in claiming his birthright but overcomes them dauntlessly to achieve his goal. Theseus and Oedipus become kings, of Athens and Thebes respectively, and the myths about them are inextricably linked with the Bronze Age prehistory of those cities. But Heracles does not mount a throne despite having links with the ruling families of various cities, Thebes and Mycenae among them. One reason may have been his very popularity: so many states wanted to establish a connection with him that he was condemned to a wandering life.

The least expected joint element in the three heroic biographies is their tragic cast. Each of the heroes starts out with all the advantages normally thought conducive to success – good looks, formidable strength, enterprise, great courage and connections to power. Yet their lives, while marked by exceptional triumphs, are also dogged by misfortune. Theseus's meteoric rise to occupy the throne of Athens is followed by a sad decline into failure and exile. Oedipus is doomed from the start, victim of a remorseless and unforgiving destiny. And Heracles, the mightiest of men, is pursued throughout his life by the wrath of the goddess Hera, who thwarts him and forces upon him the twelve labours for which he is still best remembered.

Yet the Greek view of life, although often pessimistic, was never unreservedly bleak, and in each case the mythmakers compensated their heroes with a final, dramatic apotheosis. Theseus had to wait until long after his death, but he emerged at last as Athens's supernatural champion; Oedipus's long, dark path ended in a blinding flash of light; and Heracles, the supreme hero, received the ultimate accolade when he ascended from his funeral pyre to be welcomed by his father Zeus on Mount Olympus as one of the gods.

Opposite: The feats of the hero Theseus are depicted on this red-figure kylix of *c.*440BC. In the centre, he defeats the monstrous Minotaur. At the top, he wrestles with Kerkyon. At the bottom, he slays the bull at Marathon.

Below: Heracles is depicted in his role as a superb marksman in this statue from the island of Aegina.

Theseus, King of Athens

The myth of Theseus, slayer of the Minotaur, begins like so many stories with a king's fear that he will never produce a son to inherit the throne when he dies. In the Bronze Age, the throne of Athens, capital of the kingdom of Attica, was a prize widely coveted.

King Aegeus was a worried man. His hold on the realm of Attica was under threat. Although he had married twice he remained childless, while his brother Pallas had no fewer than fifty sons who were all eager to claim the throne. In his uncertainty, the ruler decided to go to Delphi and consult the oracle to discover the best course of action. The pronouncement of the Delphic prophetess's was typically enigmatic; she told the king not to unstopper his bulging wineskin until he returned to Athens.

Unsure of her meaning, the king decided to make a detour to Troezen, a small town in the northeastern Peloponnese across the Saronic Gulf from Athens. Its ruler, Pittheus, was famous for his wisdom, and Aegeus thought that if anyone could understand the cryptic message, he could.

Indeed, Pittheus recognized the seer's words to mean that Aegeus should avoid sexual activity until he got home. But he saw a chance to win a powerful husband for his unmarried daughter Aethra and, instead of explaining the prophecy, he got his guest drunk and sent him to bed with the girl. The next morning, Aegeus realized what had happened and guessed that a son might have been conceived. He told Aethra that if she bore his child, she would have to bring him up in secret to

Foremost among Theseus's attributes was his strength. He first demonstrated his heroic stature by lifting a vast rock that concealed the tokens of his birthright.

protect him from his fifty cousins and he devised a test that would reveal the boy's identity. He buried his sword and sandals under a huge stone that only his son would be able to raise, when he had reached manhood. The boy could then travel to Athens, bringing with him Aegeus's belongings, and the king would recognize him as his heir.

Nine months later Aethra did indeed give birth to a boy, and she named him Theseus. By the time he reached sixteen, he was as strong as he was brave, and his mother decided that he was ready for the test. Lifting the rock proved no problem at all for Theseus, and he easily recovered the tokens that the king had left. Nothing could now stop the young man from setting off for Athens to claim his birthright. The city was an easy sea voyage across the gulf from Troezen, but Theseus preferred to take the longer and slower land route. He did so knowing that many perils awaited him, for the Gulf's shores were infested with brigands. He wanted to show what he could do.

Theseus's first encounter was with a ruffian called Periphetes, nicknamed "Club-clouter" for his mighty bronze-plated cudgel. Theseus wrested it from him and laid him low with it. But he was so pleased with his newly acquired weapon that he bore it throughout the rest of his career. He met his second assailant at the neck of the Isthmus of Corinth. Here lived a sadistic robber named Sinis, known as "Pine-bender" due to his habit of tying victims to bent saplings that he then released, so tearing them in two. Theseus got the better of him – and subjected the villain to the same horrible fate that he had inflicted on others.

At Krommyon on the northern shore of the gulf, Theseus killed a monstrous sow that was terrorizing the neighbourhood. Continuing along the cliffs, he ran into a brigand named Skiron, who killed travellers for sport. He commanded passers-by to wash his feet; when they bent to do so, he would kick them into the sea, where a giant turtle waited to devour them. Once again the hero gave the thug a dose of his own medicine, hurling him far into the waves to serve as food for the reptile.

Two more ordeals awaited Theseus before he reached his destination. Near Eleusis he was confronted by Kerkyon, a bone-crushing wrestler who also proved no match for the hero. Finally Theseus came to the house of Polypemon, a sinister individual who used to offer travellers accommodation only on order to rob and murder them as they slept. He killed his victims by adjusting them to the

Greece's Favourite Sport

Unarmed combat between a hero and a powerful opponent, often to the death, is a feature of many myths. Such tales reflect the importance of wrestling as ancient Greece's favourite competitive sport.

When Theseus fought Kerkyon (see above), he was practising a skill that every Greek youth would have learned in the gyms – *palaistrae*, meaning literally "wrestling-grounds". The sport took two forms. One was similar to modern wrestling. The other, known as the *pankration*, was an all-in confrontation in which only the gouging of eyes was forbidden. These bouts ended when one participant raised an arm in submission.

Famous wrestlers of the day were treated like heroes. One Milo of Kroton – who could reputedly break a cord tied round his forehead simply by dilating his blood vessels – was said to have been killed by wolves after his arm got caught in a split tree-trunk that he was trying to force apart.

The aim of the milder form of wrestling – shown in a detail from a red-figure vase – was to grip an opponent's oiled body and tumble him; three falls meant victory.

size of the bed in which they lay. Tall individuals had their feet lopped off with an axe, while the arms and legs of short people were tied to sinews and racked until they fitted the bed, a form of torture that won him the nickname of Procrustes, "The Stretcher". Theseus killed Procrustes horribly on the brigand's own bed.

When the young hero finally reached Athens his first act was to have himself purged of blood-guilt at the River Kephisos. Yet there were fresh dangers awaiting him in the city, for Athens was going through troubled times. In the years since his liaison with Aethra, King Aegeus had married again. His new wife was none other than the sorceress Medea (see pages 44–45), who had fled to Athens after leaving Jason. In the intervening years, she had borne Aegeus a son, Medus.

Through her psychic powers, Medea instantly realized that the vigorous young stranger was a rival to her son. Convincing Aegeus that he must be a spy, she persuaded the king to offer Theseus a poisoned draught of wine. At the last moment, though, Aegeus glimpsed the hilt of Theseus's sword and recognized it as the one he had hidden at Troezen. Dashing the fatal cup from the young man's lips, Aegeus proclaimed him his heir.

The announcement caused widespread rejoicing, although by no means everyone was pleased. Medea and her son fled the kingdom in despair. For the fifty sons of Pallas, who now realised that their last hope of inheriting the crown might have disappeared for good, the news was the final straw. They rose in revolt, preparing an ambush for the royal forces. But Theseus got wind of their plans and apprehended the waiting soldiers, forcing his cousins to sue for peace.

Into the Minotaur's Lair

The best known of Theseus's exploits took place on the far-off island of Crete. The island's ruler, Minos, had gone to war with Athens after his son had been killed on a visit to Attica. His troops gained the upper hand and the Athenians were forced to admit defeat. Minos imposed a harsh condition: every ninth year, seven Athenian youths and seven maidens were to be sent to Crete for an invariably fatal encounter with the hideous monster known as the Minotaur.

This freak of nature, with the body of a man and the head of a bull, was the result of an unnatural liaison between Minos's wife Pasiphae and a bull that the god Poseidon had sent from the sea. The monster had cannibalistic appetites, so to protect his subjects Minos commanded the inventor

The bull was an object of veneration in Cretan religion, although scholars are not sure exactly how it was worshipped. This 15th-century BC bull's head was found at Knossos.

Daedalus the Inventor

Daedalus, the great creative craftsman of Greek myth, was an ambivalent figure – all his best ideas had unforeseen and tragic consequences.

Daedalus was an Athenian employed by the royal house of Crete. One day, Queen Pasiphae told him a terrible secret. She confessed to feeling an unnatural lust for a white bull that Poseidon had given her husband; and she wanted the inventor's help in sating her desire.

Daedalus created a hollow wooden cow in which the queen hid herself while the beast mounted her. The result of this liaison was the Minotaur, a monster with the body of a man and a bull's head. When Minos was racking his brains to decide what to do with the creature, the inventor devised the Labyrinth – a maze-like prison – in which to confine it.

Eventually, Daedalus wanted to leave Crete, but Minos was unwilling to let him go. Knowing that the ports were guarded, the inventor decided to leave by air. He made wings out of feathers and wax for himself and his son Icarus, and the two flew away from the island together. But despite his father's warnings, Icarus could not resist soaring up towards the sun, whose heat caused the wax to melt. The feathers fell away and Icarus plummeted into the sea. He was buried on the Greek island later known as Icaria in his honour. Like his earlier exploits, Daedalus's experiment with flight had gone tragically wrong.

Daedalus (see page 53) to construct the Labyrinth, a maze in which the beast could be immured.

Before Theseus's time, two boatloads of young Athenians had been despatched to meet their fate in the creature's lair. But Theseus swore that they would be the last. Volunteering for the third party, he promised to rid the world of the Minotaur for ever. His father did everything in his power to dissuade him, but Theseus remained adamant. The ship was decked out with black sails in mourning for the victims, for none was expected to come back. Theseus did his best to cheer Aegeus by insisting that he would bring the ship home with white sails raised to show that he and his comrades were alive and well.

Arriving in Crete, the Athenians were taken to Minos's palace. There the young hero caught the attention of the ruler's daughter Ariadne, who fell in love with him at first sight and resolved to do everything in her power to save him. She soon found a means to slip him a ball of twine, whispering to him to unfurl it so that he could find a

way out of the Labyrinth. She also surreptitiously provided him with a sword. That night, when Theseus volunteered to be the Minotaur's first victim, he did so knowing he was not entirely unprotected. Even so, the angry bellowing that reached his ears from the depths of the maze must have tested his courage. But when he finally confronted the monster, his nerve did not fail him. Grappling the beast closely enough to feel the moisture of its fetid breath on his cheek, he thrust the sword into its body, killing the monster instantly.

He quickly retraced his steps through the maze, using the twine to guide him. When he emerged, Ariadne was waiting for him. She had managed to obtain keys to the prison in which the other Athenians were held, and she distracted the guards long enough to allow Theseus to free his comrades. Then she fled with the fugitives down to the harbour, where the boat that had brought them lay moored. Casting off, the party set off through the night towards Athens.

After this dramatic escape, the story of their return is something of an anticlimax – so much so that people have puzzled over its deficiencies ever since classical times. First, Theseus, for no given reason, abandoned the lovelorn Ariadne on the island of Naxos (see page 57). Then, after stopping off at nearby Delos to give thanks to the gods for his release, he had another odd lapse, forgetting his promise to his father to rig the returning ship in white. Seeing black sails flying, Aegeus, who was watching for his son's return from an eyrie on the Acropolis, assumed the worst and in his despair, jumped off the rock to his death.

Coming so soon after Theseus's desertion of Ariadne, this second failing has left scholars searching for explanations. Some have suggested that, in a lost version of the story, the hero must have broken a taboo and been punished by temporary forgetfulness. Others, noting Minos's failure

With the Minotaur slain, Theseus is greeted with a mixture of awe and astonishment in this Roman wall painting. In some versions of the myth, before Theseus left Greece for Crete he killed the Minotaur's father – a wild bull – at Marathon.

The Bulls of Minos and the Lost Labyrinth

At first hearing, the killing of the Minotaur seems like the most farfetched of all the Theseus myths. Yet archaeological discoveries made in the past century have suggested the story might have drawn on folk memories of Minoan Crete.

Excavation of the royal palace at Knossos revealed a groundplan of startling complexity: hundreds of rooms gave off corridors and passageways around a central court. To mainland Greeks – used at the time to living in simple two-room dwellings – the palace buildings may well have seemed to be a forbidding maze. A motif in the palace decorations was the labrys or double-headed axe, suggesting the building may have been dubbed the Labyrinth or "House of the Axe".

Evocative images of bulls were found on seals and frescoes painted on the palace walls. It soon became apparent that they illustrated a lost sport. The images showed spectators watching acrobats bull-leaping, an activity that involved seizing the horns of a charging bull and somersaulting over its back. There must have been

many injuries and even fatalities when things did not go according to plan. Scholars who are familiar with the Minotaur story have suggested that accounts of such deaths – perhaps involving prisoners of war – might have filtered back to the mainland and inspired the myth.

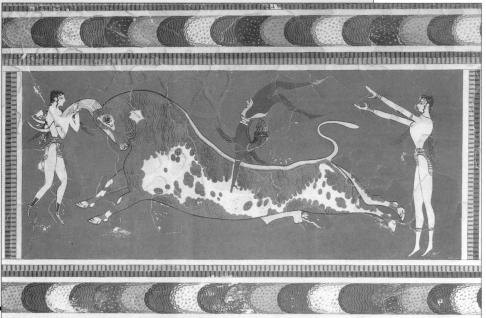

An acrobat risks his life by somersaulting over a charging bull in this reconstructed fresco at the royal palace of Knossos.

to hunt down the fugitives, have suggested that there might have been an element of magical flight – a familiar folk-tale motif in which a pursuer is held back by supernatural obstacles.

A Revered Athenian Ruler

Theseus returned to find himself King of Attica as a result of Aegeus's death, and as such he was to be honoured as a founding father by later generations of Athenians. Writers of the Classical era would praise his governance, citing innovations credited to him as precedents for policies they wished governments to pursue in their own day.

In the stories of his kingship, myth and historical reality were inextricably interwoven. For example, Theseus's chief achievement as a ruler was said to be the centralization of power in Athens. The region of Attica had previously consisted of a dozen largely self-governing communities, an arrangement that had encouraged inefficiency and strife; but Theseus persuaded the eleven smaller centres to give up some of their independence in return for an equal say in the federal government of the whole state. Some such reform did take place in the centuries before records were kept. By attributing it to Theseus, Athenians gave it incontestable authority. Yet

alongside these quasi-historical acts of governance, Theseus also continued to indulge in traditional heroics. In his youth he had modelled himself on Heracles; later he became the older hero's
friend, helping him in his ninth labour when he
raided the land of the Amazons (see page 71).

Athenian propaganda also played a part in
this tale. Early accounts of the episode treated it as
an amorous escapade in which Theseus's principal aim was to carry off the Amazonian queen,
variously called Antiope or Hippolyte. But later
writers, influenced by Athens's struggle with Per-
sia in the fifth century BC, put a patriotic slant on
the myth. In their retelling, the Amazons became
the aggressors, invading Athens itself. Theseus
now became a national hero resisting the proto-
types of subsequent Asian invaders. Both versions
of the story ended with an Athenian victory sealed
by Theseus's marriage to the Amazon queen, who
bore him a son, Hippolytus.

But Theseus's adventures did
not always have such propitious
outcomes. His friendship with
Peirithous, ruler of the Lapith
people of Thessaly, was to
involve him in deep trouble. As
chance would have it, the first
time they met Peirithous was
about to be married, and to seal
the new friendship, he invited
Theseus to the wedding. Among
the other guests was a party of
centaurs, creatures with the heads
and torsoes of men but the
hindquarters of horses (see pages
76–77). These semi-socialized
beings were not used to drinking
wine, and the alcohol that flowed
freely at the feast soon went to
their heads. The result was that when the bride
came to greet them, their leader seized her by the
hair and dragged her into the bushes. Others followed his example, snatching maidens and boys
at random. Peirithous leaped to his wife's defence,
with Theseus at his side. The centaurs were
beaten – expelled from the feast and driven out of
their hunting grounds on Mount Pelion.

But marriage apparently did little to curb
Peirithous's own libido, for he subsequently
involved Theseus in two amatory exploits that had
disastrous consequences. The first involved the
celebrated Helen, whose abduction by Paris
would later lead to the Siege of Troy (see pages
84–85). She was still only a young girl when the
two kings set out to abduct her, bringing her back
from Sparta to Attica where, because she was not
yet of marriageable age, they left her under the
protection of Theseus's mother Aethra. Helen's
family responded quickly. Her twin brothers

Ariadne on Naxos

Having given up home and family to help Theseus, Ariadne found herself abandoned on a remote island, the very archetype of the deserted woman. But her story had a happy ending: her plight was noted on Olympus, and a god came to the rescue.

Ariadne lies abandoned by Theseus in this Roman sculpture. The garland she later wore at her wedding became the Northern Crown constellation.

Ariadne's decision to help Theseus overcome the Minotaur meant that she had to betray her father's trust and leave her home. She acted under the illusion that the young hero would take her back to Athens and marry her there.

But she was cruelly disappointed. On reaching the island of Dia – identified by most scholars with modern Naxos, though some plump for the small island of Dia just off Crete's north coast – he abandoned her. While she slept on shore, he and his comrades sailed away, leaving her to a bitter awakening alone in a strange land.

Luckily, the Olympians heard her complaints, and Dionysus himself came to her rescue. The god of wine arrived on the island accompanied by a festive train of satyrs and maenads. He informed the startled maiden that he had come to marry her forthwith, telling her "Your wedding present is the sky itself!"

The two went back to Olympus, where over the years Ariadne was to bear her divine husband many children. In later times her story would attract the attention of great artists. The sixteenth-century Italian Titian painted a celebrated "Bacchus and Ariadne"; Bacchus was Dionysus's Roman name. In the twentieth century, German composer Richard Strauss composed the opera *Ariadne auf Naxos*, a modern favourite.

Castor and Pollux raised an army and invaded Attica in search of her. They bore Helen back to Sparta, taking Aethra along with them.

Theseus was unable to respond because Peirithous had involved him in another debacle. The Lapith ruler had decided to seduce Persephone, daughter of Zeus and Demeter and wife of Hades, ruler of the Underworld. He persuaded Theseus to accompany him. So the two entered the Underworld through a cavern and boldly made their way to the dread lord's palace. By his divine prescience, Hades was aware of the purpose of their visit, but he feigned hospitality when they arrived, offering them a couch to sit on. They accepted gratefully, not realizing until it was too late that they were lowering themselves onto the Seat of Forgetfulness, which melded itself into their flesh, preventing them from rising.

Theseus remained trapped there for four years and might have stayed for ever had Heracles not passed by on his quest for the guard dog Cerberus (see page 74). The hero rescued him, but was unable to do the same for Peirithous, who as a mere mortal was condemned to eternal seclusion for his effrontery in trying to abduct a goddess.

Father Turns against Son

Theseus returned, chastened, to Athens. He was an old man by now and a widower, for his Amazon bride had died during his absence. Looking around for a new wife, he settled on Phaedra, the sister of the same Ariadne he had deserted so long ago. Perhaps the match was ill-starred from the start. It certainly had tragic consequences, for the new queen soon fell in love with her son-in-law Hippolytus, Theseus's child by his previous wife. The young man rejected her advances, and in despair she hanged herself – but not before writing a letter to Theseus that falsely accused Hippolytus of trying to violate her.

In a fury of grief, the old king cursed his son for the tragedy he had brought about. Then, remembering that Poseidon had once granted him three wishes, he used one to beg the god to punish Hippolytus. The Olympian responded at once, sending a sea monster to confront the youth. It caught up with him as he was mounting a chariot to flee his father's wrath. Seized by panic at the sight, the horses bolted and Hippolytus was dragged behind them, entangled in the reins.

Meanwhile Theseus had learned the truth, revealed to him – according to the play by the fifth-century BC Greek dramatist Euripides – by the goddess Artemis who loved Hippolytus for his chastity. Theseus went off in search of his son, only to find him dying. Although the two enjoyed a death-bed reconciliation, it came as little consolation to the old king. The career that had begun so gloriously now seemed doomed to end in misery and failure.

The onset of the final act was abrupt. A rebel faction challenged Theseus's rule and forced him to abdicate the throne. The deposed king escaped by ship to Skyros, where he owned an estate. The island's ruler made a show of welcoming him. In fact, however, he was far from pleased to see the Athenian, as he had long since taken to treating the absent king's land as his own. Under the pretence of showing him the boundaries of his estates, he inveigled Theseus to the top of a high cliff and pushed him off to his death. Subsequently he claimed that the old man had stumbled and fallen accidentally. In this sordid way the fearless conqueror of the Minotaur met his death.

Over the centuries, however, he came to be remembered not for his sad later years, but for the great triumphs of his youth. In the fifth century BC, when Athens was confronting the Persian threat, the long-dead hero was reportedly seen in full armour at the decisive Battle of Marathon, fighting alongside the Athenian forces. A few decades after the sighting, the Athenian statesman Cimon courted popularity with his fellow citizens by sending an expedition to Skyros in search of the hero's grave. It returned with some ancient remains that were reburied with full ceremonial honours in the Theseum, a specially built mausoleum. In the eyes of his fellow countrymen, Theseus had come home at last.

**Theseus's handsome son Hippolytus
seems unshocked by the advances of his father's new
young wife Phaedra in this Roman tomb relief.**

Oedipus and the Tragedy of Thebes

No royal house was so accursed as that of the Greek city of Thebes: each generation suffered a peculiar kind of tragedy. But of all the city's rulers the quick-witted foundling prince Oedipus was condemned by the gods to the most terrible fate.

Just as Theseus was the hero of Athens, so Oedipus's tragic fate was indissolubly linked with Thebes, the capital of the state of Boeotia on Attica's northern border. The Theban saga began, like so many others, with one of Zeus's love affairs. In this case the object of the god's attentions was Europa, daughter of the King of Phoenicia. To seduce her, Zeus disguised himself as a huge white bull. When he had persuaded her to climb on his back he plunged into the sea and headed off across the Mediterranean. Europa's father dispatched his son Cadmus to find her, telling him not to return without her.

Cadmus travelled the world for years without success and went to Delphi to ask the oracle if he would ever be able to end his quest. The prophetess told him to give up the search for his sister, and instead watch out for a portent: a cow that had never been yoked, which he would meet in a deserted spot. He should follow this beast as far as it chose to go, then found a city on the spot where it settled. Cadmus did as he was told and thereby laid the foundations of Thebes. Later the gods gave him Harmonia, the daughter of Ares and Aphrodite, as a wife, and the couple were blessed with four daughters.

When the Theban prince Actaeon spotted the goddess Artemis (left) bathing, she swore to take revenge.

For a time Cadmus must have thought himself the luckiest man alive. Yet terrible misfortune was destined to befall his house. First, his daughter Semele attracted the notice of Zeus and, as a result, she became pregnant with Dionysus, the future god of wine. Zeus's jealous consort, Hera, learned of the affair and destroyed the girl (see box, page 27). Next, tragedy struck a grandson of Cadmus called Actaeon. He was a hunter who spent all his spare time in the mountains. There he stumbled upon Artemis bathing naked with her nymphs in a sacred grove. The virgin goddess instantly resolved to punish his unintentional sacrilege with death, so she changed him into a stag and set his own hounds on him.

The fate of Pentheus, the son of Cadmus's second daughter Agave, was equally horrible. He inherited the kingdom from his grandfather and for a while enjoyed an era of peace. It was during his reign, however, that the worship of Dionysus reached Boeotia. Pentheus opposed the new religion and did everything in his power to suppress the rites performed by the god's followers. In so doing he attracted the anger of Dionysus himself. When he went in person to Mount Cithaeron where the worshippers gathered, Dionysus so maddened his devotees that they fell upon the intruder and tore him limb from limb. His own mother wrenched the king's head from his body.

Such was the grim destiny of the house of Cadmus. With the destruction of its second generation, the throne of Thebes passed to Pentheus's cousin Laius. But the shadow that had fallen on the family remained, and the Fates had further horrors in store for the next generation. Laius married Jocasta, also a member of the Cadmian royal house. When she bore him a baby boy, the

Zeus, in the form of a white bull, carries Europa off to Crete, in
this Roman mosaic. Her father Agenor can only watch in
dismay, but it was his response – sending Cadmus on the quest
to recover Europa – that resulted in the foundation of Thebes.

parents' joy was soured by an oracle which warned that Laius would one day be killed by his own son. Fearing for his life, the king had a spike driven through the feet of the infant and gave orders for it to be abandoned on Mount Cithaeron.

But the attendant entrusted with the task did not have the heart to leave the baby and instead gave him to a herdsman in the service of Polybus, ruler of Corinth. Knowing that the king and his wife Merope were childless, he left the infant at the palace. The royal couple adopted the child, giving him the name of Oedipus – "Swollen Feet".

Over the years the lameness passed and, by the time he reached adulthood, Oedipus was a worthy scion of the royal house. His accomplishments roused the envy of other courtiers, one of whom told him that he was not his parents' son. Oedipus confronted Merope, who replied evasively, so he decided to consult the Delphic oracle. But when he asked her who he was, she recoiled from him, telling him he was fated to kill his father and marry his own mother.

Oedipus decided not to return to Corinth and risk harming those he loved. Instead he took the road to Thebes. At a crossroads he met a party of travellers, including a man being carried in a litter. A guard thrust a staff at Oedipus, telling him to make way. Oedipus was not used to such treatment – and, overcome with fury, he killed the guard. Seeing their comrade struck down, the rest of the party fell on his attacker. Within minutes Oedipus had killed them all. The last to die was the old man – his true father Laius.

Meanwhile, in Thebes a terrible monster called the Sphinx was waylaying travellers outside the city, demanding that they answer a riddle. When they failed to do so, despite their best efforts, she killed them. King Laius himself had set out to Delphi in order to ask the oracle how to rid his kingdom of this pest.

Oedipus confronts the riddling Sphinx in this image from a Greek vase of the 5th century BC. In the Oedipus myth, the monster – whose name means "the strangler" – throttled the unlucky Thebans who failed to answer its question correctly.

When word of the king's death filtered back to Thebes, it was announced that any man who could solve the riddle would win the hand of the widowed Queen Jocasta and become the new king. Oedipus jumped at the chance and immediately went to find the Sphinx. The creature sat waiting on the tip of a pillar of rock that towered over the road. She gazed at him unblinkingly as he approached, and when he asked to know the riddle intoned: "What is it that walks on four legs in the morning, on two legs at noon and in the evening on three?" "Human beings," Oedipus replied. "They crawl on hands and knees as infants in the morning of their lives. Growing up, they walk on two legs, but in old age they need a stick for support, as if they had three legs."

It was the right answer. With a cry of anguish, the Sphinx hurled herself from the roadside eyrie down to her death. Oedipus had delivered Thebes from its tormentor, so he was welcomed into the city and proclaimed as the new king. Jocasta was waiting to meet him, and soon the two were man and wife. The prophecy was fulfilled.

Oedipus went on to rule Thebes well, and the kingdom prospered. He and Jocasta had children: twin sons Eteocles and Polynices, and two daughters, Antigone and Ismene. But one day plague struck the realm. Cattle died in the fields and the crops were blighted. Stunned by this sudden reversal of fortune, Oedipus sent a messenger to Delphi to ask the oracle why his kingdom was being punished in this way. The reply came back that

Mistress of Enigma

The Sphinx is one of the most mysterious of the Greek monsters. Her riddle and her chilling smile captured the imagination of later generations. Like the other monsters, she may have been adopted from an older religion.

A winged creature with the head of a woman and the body of a lion, the Sphinx was the ghastly daughter of the monsters Echidna and Typhon. She flew to Thebes all the way from Ethiopia, dispatched by the goddess Hera to plague the city because King Laius had abducted a boy, Chrysippus – an offence against the goddess of marriage. In another version the Sphinx was sent by Apollo or Dionysus to punish the Thebans for failing to worship the gods properly. Some say the Sphinx was taught her question by the Three Muses, goddesses of the arts. The poet Robert Graves has suggested that she represented an ancient mother goddess worshipped before the Olympians.

A Greek marble carving gives the Sphinx an inscrutable gaze. Her hybrid body combines beauty and strength.

63

Thebes could expect no respite until Laius's killer had been discovered and expelled.

Little suspecting the consequences of his action, Oedipus flung himself energetically into the task of investigating the death. He summoned the blind prophet Tiresias (see page 67), whose reputation for wisdom was unmatched. The seer was reluctant to tell the terrible truth but under pressure finally revealed that Oedipus himself had murdered King Laius at the crossroads years ago.

Trembling, Oedipus called for Jocasta and quizzed her about the clothes that Laius and his attendants had been wearing that fateful day. She tried to reassure him, suggesting that prophets were sometimes wrong. As proof, she cited her own experience: an oracle had once foretold that Laius would be killed by his own son, a manifest impossibility since his only child had died in infancy on the slopes of Mount Cithaeron.

Oedipus had never heard this story, and now he insisted on learning every detail. Deeply troubled, he gave orders for the attendant who had taken the child to the mountain to be summoned. Eventually a very old man was led in and he confessed that he had passed his burden on to a herdsman who had ensured that the boy was raised in the palace at Corinth.

As the truth began finally to dawn on Oedipus, a blood-curdling cry rang out from elsewhere in the palace. Running to see what had happened, he found Jocasta dead. On learning the news, she had hanged herself. In despair, Oedipus plucked a buckle from her girdle and used the pin to put out his eyes. Blind and with nothing other than the clothes he wore, he blundered out of the palace and left his kingdom on foot, to wander the world in search of atonement.

After many years, he came at last to Theseus's Attica. He was received kindly there, not least because an oracle had foreseen peace and prosperity for the country in which he died. So he settled at last in the little town of Colonus, not far from Athens, and waited for the end.

When death came for him at last, it did so in miraculous fashion. Only Theseus was with Oedipus in the final hour. As though in a trance he made his way to the predestined spot, whose exact location was afterwards known only to Theseus and his successor kings. As Oedipus stood there, Zeus sent a thunderclap, and Theseus covered his eyes in fear and reverence. When he opened them again, Oedipus was gone.

Antigone's Tragic Defiance

Even with Oedipus's death, the sorrows of the Theban royal house were not over. The drama of his daughter was the subject of the play Antigone *by the fifth-century BC dramatist Sophocles.*

After Oedipus's death, his two sons quarrelled over the succession to the throne. Eventually they decided to rule in alternate years. Eteocles took the first turn, but when his time was up he refused to hand over the kingdom to his brother as promised.

Polynices raised an army to enforce his claim, sharing command with six allied leaders – the famous Seven against Thebes. But their forces were driven back from the city with huge losses. Both Oedipus's sons were killed in a duel. With their deaths, the throne reverted to their uncle Creon.

Creon's first thought was to deter future rebels. So he gave orders that, while Eteocles should be interred in state as Thebes's former ruler, his brother Polynices

Battlefield honour was cast aside by Creon when he refused burial to the warrior Polynices, provoking Antigone's rage. This classical period plaque depicts a line of soldiers.

should be left unburied. He decreed that those who disobeyed would die.

Even so, one person was determined to defy the king's will. That night, Polynices's sister Antigone visited the battlefield and found her brother's body. She covered it with earth, giving him a proper burial. Caught in the act, the princess was taken to her uncle, who upbraided her. She refused to apologize, citing the demands of divine law in her defence. She refused to concede to the king even when he condemned her to death.

The cruelty of the sentence shocked Thebes, but Creon refused all appeals for mercy. Only when the old prophet Tiresias warned the king that the gods would punish him for the deed did Creon finally consider clemency.

But his change of heart came too late: he found that the princess had hanged herself with her veil. In despair at the death of his beloved, Haemon, Creon's son, threw himself onto his sword, dying instantly, and when Creon's wife Eurydice learned of her son's suicide, she too stabbed herself fatally.

In this Etruscan carving, Oedipus, between his devastated sons, turns blindly towards a bleak future after he has put out his own eyes. In some tellings of the myth he did not go at once into exile but stayed for many years in Thebes and cursed his sons after a quarrel.

65

The Labours of Heracles

The Greek hero Heracles – known to the Romans as Hercules – had no match for strength or courage. Yet unrelenting animosity from the goddess Hera ensured that his life was dogged by trials, and other people benefited from his deeds more than he did.

Heracles was the son of Zeus and Alcmene, a granddaughter of Perseus. Overcome with desire for the mortal woman, Zeus came to her in the form of her intended, Amphitryon, and stretched the night of their lovemaking to three times its normal length to increase his pleasure. Alcmene was puzzled when the following day the true Amphitryon arrived back from a journey; the couple only learned the truth when the blind prophet Tiresias revealed the trick that Zeus had played.

Nine months later, Alcmene gave birth to twins, Heracles and Iphikles. Zeus, who was determined that the first-born should not just be the mightiest of men but also eventually a god, tricked the goddess Hera into breast-feeding the new-born baby, thereby suckling him on the milk of immortality. But the lusty infant drew so forcefully on the proffered nipple that Hera pulled away in pain, and some of the milk spattered across the sky, where it became the band of stars still known as the Milky Way. When she learned that the infant who had caused her such pain was also Zeus's illegitimate son, her anger escalated and she became the future hero's lifelong enemy.

Heracles was still in his cradle when she first tried to get her own back. In an attempt to kill the twins, she sent two serpents into their bedroom as they lay sleeping. But the young hero's strength was already phenomenal, and when his parents rushed in to find the cause of the commotion, they found the infant proudly holding up the dead

Heracles's great physical presence is emphasized in this Greek statue of the 1st century BC. Yet his qualities of strength and endurance were undermined by vices – several times he was undone by his violent temper and his lust for women.

Tiresias the Prophet

Tiresias was no ordinary mortal. He lived for seven lifespans, in the course of which he spent time as a woman as well as a man. Even after death, he alone of the shades in Hades's realm was allowed to retain the gifts of speech and understanding, enabling him to continue his role as a prophet.

Tiresias's first transformation took place one day on Mount Kyllene, where he saw two snakes coupling. He struck them with his staff, killing the female. Instantly he found himself transformed into a woman. Seven years later, he saw another pair of snakes similarly occupied. This time he dispatched the male, and was turned back into a man.

Some time later, Zeus and Hera were arguing over which partner gets the most pleasure from the sexual act, and to settle the dispute they decided to consult the one person on Earth to have had experience of both conditions. Tiresias replied that, judged out of ten, the female gets nine parts of the enjoyment and the man only one – an answer that so infuriated Hera that she struck him blind on the spot. In consolation, Zeus bestowed upon him the gifts of long life and of prophecy.

Subsequently Tiresias became famous equally for his great age and for his ability to foresee the future. He played a vital part in the Oedipus saga (see page 64), was consulted by the parents of Heracles, and gave crucial advice to the rulers of Thebes during two successive sieges. Even after his death his prophetic powers were not silenced. In the *Odyssey* Homer describes how Odysseus went to consult him in the land of the dead to learn the outcome of his long homeward journey.

Debates between Zeus and Hera, as depicted in this 5th-century BC carving, kept the gods amused. Tiresias was consulted to settle one such dispute.

snakes. Thereafter Hera never again tried directly to kill him; instead she used more subtle means to bring about his destruction.

Heracles's childhood was happy and for the most part uneventful. He grew up more skilled in archery, swordplay, boxing and wrestling than any other mortal; and he also learned the arts of singing and music-making. Yet his temper was fierce and, when coupled with his great strength, soon got him into trouble. A music teacher struck him for playing false notes and he retaliated so violently that the man died. Though he was

pardoned, he was nonetheless sent away from his parents' home to tend herds on Mount Cithaeron. Here Heracles faced his first real challenge when he tracked down a fierce lion that had been savaging cattle. He killed the beast with an olivewood cudgel, skinned it and made a cloak out of its pelt. In time the club and the lionskin worn over his shoulder would become his trademarks.

As he was returning to his home in Thebes, he fell in with heralds from the nearby city of Orchomenus. Heracles asked them the reason for their journey. They had come, they explained, to claim the annual tribute that the Thebans paid to their ruler, the king of the Minyan people. The tribute, the heralds said, reflected the Thebans' gratitude to the Minyan king for refraining from slicing off their hands, ears and noses. Heracles was outraged and he treated the heralds in just the way they had described, sending them back to their master horribly mutilated. Inevitably, the deed led to war between the two peoples. Heracles led the Thebans and vanquished the Minyans almost single-handedly, killing their arrogant king. He returned to Thebes a hero, and the Theban monarch rewarded him with the hand of his own daughter, the princess Megara.

So began the happiest period of Heracles's life. He and his wife had three sons, and he lived quietly with his family, expecting to inherit the throne of Thebes when the old king died. But Hera had not forgotten her grudge. Now she struck, making Heracles insane so that he mistook his own sons for enemies and killed them. On hearing the news, Megara died of a broken heart.

Heracles Seeks a Penance

When he came to his senses again and realized what he had done, Heracles at first lost the will to live. Then he determined to go to Delphi to ask Apollo's priestess if there was any way in which he could atone for the terrible crime he had committed. The prophetess gave him clear instructions: he was to leave for Tiryns, in the territory of his cousin Eurystheus, King of Mycenae, whose service he must enter; and he must remain there for an unspecified length of time, performing whatever labours the ruler demanded of him. If he did so, he would be rewarded with immortality. Eager

Heracles overpowers the fearsome Nemean lion in this Greek carving. After its death Zeus put the lion in the night sky as the constellation Leo.

to make amends, the hero accepted his abasement.

Eurystheus was far from pleased to see Heracles, for the newcomer had royal blood in his veins; his earthly father Amphitryon had once been King of Mycenae, but had been deposed when he accidentally killed a relative. Eurystheus sensed the presence of a rival. But he saw in the labours that Heracles had sworn to perform a heaven-sent chance to rid himself of the upstart. The fearful ruler racked his brains for a challenge likely to prove fatal, and came up with an idea: the Nemean lion.

This fearsome beast was invulnerable to weapons, and was terrorizing a mountainous district just to the north of Mycenae. When Heracles had tracked it down, he first tried firing arrows at it, but found that they rebounded from its pelt. Then he battered it with his club, which failed to wound the animal but drove it back into its cave. Realizing that he would have to use his bare hands, Heracles entered the beast's lair and wrestled with the lion, eventually throttling it. He tried to skin it, but his sword would not penetrate its flesh. Finally he used the

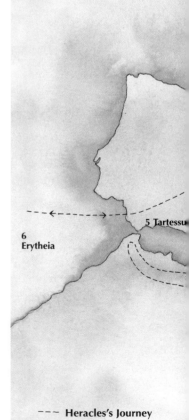

5 Tartessu

6 Erytheia

--- Heracles's Journey

beast's own claws to remove the pelt, which he wore in place of his old lionskin. Eurystheus was less than pleased to see Heracles return safely. In terror, he realized that any man who could kill such a beast would have very little trouble disposing of him, so he had an enormous brass jar made in which he could shelter while Heracles was in his palace. Henceforward, all his instructions to the hero were delivered by his herald.

Eurystheus had great hopes that the next task he had in mind would finish Heracles off. This time he instructed the hero to go to Lerna, at the head of the Gulf of Argos fifty kilometres south-west of Mycenae. There he had to kill the Hydra, a venomous nine-headed water snake.

Taking Iphicles's son Iolaus with him as a helper, Heracles made his way carefully through the marshes where the creature lived. On the advice of the goddess Athene, he forced it into the open by firing burning arrows into its lair, then set about the monster with his club. But every time he succeeded in crushing one of the writhing heads, two more instantly grew in its place. And to make matters worse, the commotion attracted the attention of an enormous crab, which emerged from the slime and seized the hero's foot in its pincers.

A powerful cudgel-blow soon dealt with that problem, but the Hydra itself proved harder to handle. Then Heracles had a brainwave. Shouting to Iolaus to pass him a lighted torch, he used the brand to sear the flesh each time he crushed one of the heads so that no new growth could force its way through. The ruse worked, and before long

Over the centuries, scholars have plotted various different routes for Heracles. Apollodorus (*c.*3rd century BC) mapped this route, which – somewhat unusually – puts the Gardens of the Hesperides in the North instead of the West.

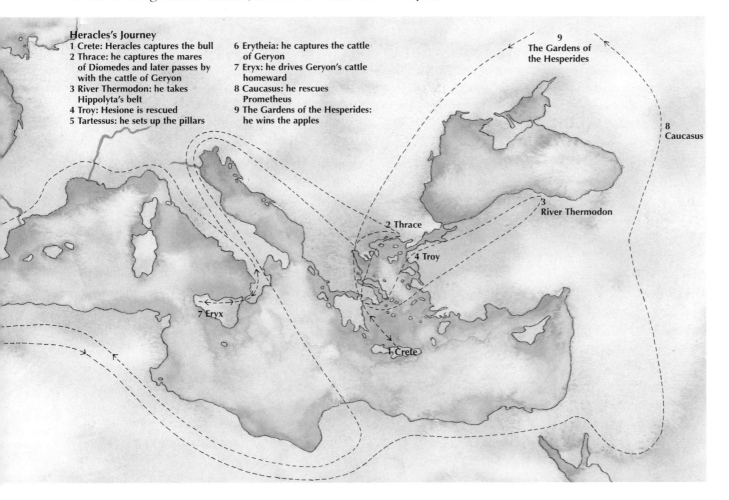

Heracles's Journey
1 **Crete:** Heracles captures the bull
2 **Thrace:** he captures the mares of Diomedes and later passes by with the cattle of Geryon
3 **River Thermodon:** he takes Hippolyta's belt
4 **Troy:** Hesione is rescued
5 **Tartessus:** he sets up the pillars
6 **Erytheia:** he captures the cattle of Geryon
7 **Eryx:** he drives Geryon's cattle homeward
8 **Caucasus:** he rescues Prometheus
9 **The Gardens of the Hesperides:** he wins the apples

9
The Gardens of the Hesperides

8
Caucasus

3
River Thermodon

2 Thrace

4 Troy

7 Eryx

1 Crete

only the central head remained. Athene had warned him that this one was immortal, so he lopped it off with his sword and then buried it under a great boulder. Before leaving the spot, Heracles dipped his arrowheads in the dead monster's poison-glands. Now they were doubly lethal, for there was no known antidote for the venom.

Eurystheus was dismissive of this exploit, claiming Heracles had cheated by calling on Iolaus for help. He next sent him off to capture the Ceryneian Hind, a deer of extraordinary beauty with golden antlers and bronze hooves. This labour tested Heracles's fleetness of foot; the hero chased it for a whole year before finally catching it and bringing it back unharmed to Mycenae.

For his fourth task, Heracles had to bring back another beast alive. This one was an enormous boar that lived on the slopes of Mount Erymanthus. The hero chased his prey into a snowdrift, where it became trapped, then carried it in fetters back to Eurystheus.

The fifth labour took Heracles beyond Mount Erymanthus to Elis, near the western coast of the Peloponnese. The ruler of the city, King Augeas, was famous for his huge herd of cattle, but the byres in which the beasts were kept had never been cleaned. Heracles's orders were to clear out many years' accumulation of dung in a single day.

Before undertaking the task, the hero approached Augeas and asked for a tenth of his herd in return for the service. The king agreed, whereupon Heracles dug trenches to divert the course of two nearby rivers through the cattle yards. Once they had been swept clean by the flood, he staunched the flow with embankments, returning the streams to their normal courses. But when he went to the king for his reward, Augeas refused payment, saying that it was the rivers that had really done the work. This was a snub that Heracles was not to forget.

The next labour that Eurystheus had planned for Heracles lay closer to hand. In the Stymphalian Marshes to the northwest of Mycenae dwelt a fearsome flock of birds. The creatures had brazen wings, claws and beaks, and they fed on human flesh. Eurystheus demanded that Heracles eradicate the fearsome flock. To exterminate the birds, Heracles made use of a bronze rattle fashioned by the god Hephaestos himself. The noise it made was so awful that the birds rose in droves, and the hero was able to use his legendary marksmanship with the bow to shoot them on the wing.

Heracles Travels Further

The first six labours had all been performed within the Peloponnese, but for the seventh Eurystheus looked further afield. At the time, the island of Crete was being plagued by the white bull from the sea that had fathered the Minotaur (see pages 52–54). Heracles's task was to rid the island of the scourge and bring the bull back alive. He managed the feat without difficulty and carried it back to Eurystheus, who only just had time to jump into his jar as it ran through the palace. He quickly instructed Heracles to set it free.

By now Eurystheus was hard put to find suitable challenges anywhere in the Greek heartland, so for the next task he dispatched the hero to faraway Thrace on the northern shores of the Aegean Sea. Word had reached Mycenae of a ruler called Diomedes who had four mares that fed on human flesh. Heracles's task was to fetch and tame these terrible creatures.

To aid him in his quest, Heracles called on the aid of a band of volunteers. Landing on the coast, they hurried to the royal stables, where they quickly overpowered the grooms. But the alarm had been raised, and as they were driving the mares back to the ships, the king himself rode out behind them at the head of the palace guard.

Thinking quickly, Heracles drove the horses to the top of a small knoll, leaving them in the charge of Abderus, one of his comrades. Then, with the rest of his men, he rushed to a sea dyke and tore a channel through it, so water poured on to the low-lying plain. Diomedes's men fled, with Heracles charging through the flood in pursuit. He captured the king and, raising him above his head, strode back with him to the knoll where the horses were waiting. There he found a terrible sight. In their panic as the waters rose, the mares had knocked Abderus down and eaten him. In his anger and grief, Heracles tossed the king to the still-hungry beasts, and he too was devoured.

With their appetites sated, the mares became tractable, and it was an easy job to herd them on to the ship. Heracles and his men sailed back to Mycenae with them, and by the time they reached Eurystheus's court the animals were quite tame. The king mated them with his own stallions, and the foals they bore were said to be Greece's finest.

Heracles's next task took him still further afield, through the Bosphorus to the southern shores of the Black Sea, the home of the fabled Amazons (see page 75). Eurystheus's daughter Admete coveted a famous girdle given to the Amazons' queen, Hippolyte, by the war god Ares. The hero's job was to bring the belt back for her.

Once more Heracles sailed with a band of comrades – among them Theseus and Peleus, the future father of Achilles. When they reached the Amazonian shore, Queen Hippolyte was so taken with the famous hero that she offered him her belt as a love-gift. But his old enemy Hera set to work, spreading a rumour among the queen's subjects that the strangers had come to abduct her. Incensed, the Amazons took to arms and a fierce battle ensued. The women warriors fought bravely, and the Greeks were hard-pressed. But in the thick of battle, Heracles seized Hippolyte's sister, Melanippe, and threatened to kill her unless his men

Eurystheus cowers in the brass jar he used as a hiding place as Heracles lifts the sturdy Erymanthian boar high over his head. The virgin goddess Athene watches (right), in this 6th-century BC Greek vase decoration. After this labour Heracles briefly joined Jason's quest for the Golden Fleece (see pages 38–40).

Single Combat with Death

A chance visit to an old friend's palace on the way to fetch Diomedes's mares from Thrace presented Heracles with one of his most daunting challenges. Determined to save the virtuous wife of the dying king, he had to confront nothing less than Death himself.

When Heracles visited his friend Admetus, king of Pherae, he was saddened to learn that the king's wife Alcestis was close to death. He was even more disturbed when he learned that she had wished her demise upon herself, hoping by it to save the life of her husband, who was mortally ill. The god Apollo had promised to revive the king if someone else would die in his place. Alcestis was the only person who had proved willing to make the sacrifice.

Hearing this, Heracles determined to save her. He stood by her side waiting for Death to arrive, and when the dreaded god came he challenged him to a wrestling match. Death accepted willingly enough, for he had never before been bested, but not even he could match the strength of Heracles. After a long struggle, he was forced to submit and leave without his victim. So Alcestis was saved, and the hero went on his way with the gratitude of the king ringing in his ears.

Hades, god of Death, bursts out of his Underworld realm in order to carry Alcestis away with him. But he has not reckoned with Heracles.

were allowed to depart unharmed. The Amazons fell back, and the raiders were able to regain their ship and slip away, carrying the Hippolyta's precious girdle with them.

Sailing back through the Dardanelles into the Aegean Sea, Heracles came across a remarkable sight: a naked maiden chained to a rock and crying piteously. Putting ashore to free her, Heracles learned that she was Hesione, daughter of King Laomedon of Troy, and that she had been left there as a sacrifice to a fearful sea monster sent by the god Poseidon to ravage the district.

Returning Hesione to her father, Heracles offered to rid the region of the scourge. In return for the service, he asked for the pair of immortal, snow-white horses that were said to have been given to Laomedon by Zeus himself. The king readily agreed, and the hero prepared for battle.

The monster proved a formidable adversary, and Heracles was eventually only able to dispatch it by climbing into its gaping jaws and hewing at its intestines from inside. When he emerged, Laomedon came to congratulate him and presented him with the horses. But one glance was enough to persuade Heracles that these were mortal beasts, not the divine ones he had been promised. He had been cheated and swore that he would be revenged on Troy's deceitful ruler.

The last three labours had taken Heracles far to the north, south and east, but now Eurystheus determined to send him to the mystic west, the least-charted destination of all. The world with which the Greeks were familiar extended no further than the Mediterranean; what lay beyond was uncertain, though some claimed that the Isles of the Blessed, where fortunate people went after death, were there. For his tenth labour, Heracles was sent to steal the cattle of Geryon, an ogre with three heads who lived on the island of Eurytheia somewhere in the uncharted Atlantic Ocean. His route took him to the mouth of the Mediterranean, which he marked by building two vast piles of stone on the north and south shores. To this day they are known as the Pillars of Hercules, the Romanized version of the hero's name.

While Heracles was working, Helios the sun god shone down on him so fiercely that the sweating hero eventually loosed an arrow at him. When the god reprimanded him, Heracles apologized and unstrung his bow. In return, Helios lent him his golden goblet, and in this vessel the hero was able to sail magically to his destination. There, he obtained the cattle after killing Geryon, whose three necks he shot with arrows.

Heracles Herds the Cattle to Greece

After returning Helios's goblet, Heracles began a long and weary journey overland back to Greece, driving the cattle before him. When he finally arrived, it was only to find that he was expected to set off westwards once more. He had to locate the Garden of the Hesperides, Mother Earth's wedding gift to Hera, and bring from it some golden apples. It was a labour in itself to find where the garden lay, for no mortal knew. Eventually he learned from Nereus, the Old Man of the Sea, that he could only hope to obtain the fruit by seeking the help of Atlas, the giant who held up the sky. Atlas proved a willing helper, for the Hesperides whom Hera had

Heracles grapples with the sea monster that threatened the Trojan king, Laomedon, from a vase of c.500 BC. The sea god Poseidon had sent the monster because Laomedon had tried to get out of paying the god for building the walls of Troy.

73

appointed to guard the garden were his daughters. He offered to fetch the apples himself if only Heracles would take over his burden.

The hero put his shoulders to the sky while Atlas went in search of the apples. But the Titan was so relieved to be free of its backbreaking weight that, when he finally returned with the fruit, he proved unwilling to swap places again. To persuade him to do so, Heracles employed a ruse, asking him to bear its weight momentarily while he adjusted his position. Atlas agreed, and Heracles beat a hasty retreat, leaving the giant to rue for all eternity his small act of kindness.

Voyage to the Underworld

For Heracles's twelfth and last labour, Eurystheus set a challenge that recalled the promise of immortality made to the hero as a reward for completing his long servitude. This time his destination was nowhere on Earth; he must visit the land of the dead. His task was to go into the Underworld realm of the dark lord Hades and bring back to Eurystheus its triple-headed guard dog, Cerberus.

After partaking of the Eleusinian Mysteries which prepared men for the experience of Hades's domain, Heracles called on the help of Athene and Hermes to guide him down into the subterranean darkness. There he rescued Theseus from bondage (see page 58) before encountering Hades himself, who grimly consented to let him borrow Cerberus if he could master the beast without recourse to weapons. The sight of the monstrous creature, its three heads maned with serpents, would have deterred a lesser man, but Heracles gripped it in an armlock, relying on his impenetrable lionskin to protect him from its gnashing jaws.

When the animal finally yielded, Heracles bound it and dragged it to the upper world, where the foam that slavered from its mouth congealed to form the plant known as deadly nightshade. The sight of this hound from Hell terrified Eurystheus more than anything he had yet seen, and he was very glad to release Heracles formally from his servitude and bid him be gone for ever.

Having returned Cerberus as promised to the Styx's shore, Heracles strode joyfully out into the sunshine, a free man at last. Yet although his long time of trial was over, there was still unfinished business remaining from the labours. In the years that followed, Heracles would return to Troy to punish the deceitful King Laomedon, and to Elis, where he would depose Augeas and sack the city.

He would use the booty from the raid on Elis to found a four-yearly festival at nearby Olympia in honour of his father Zeus. This was the prototype of the Olympic Games, re-established in historical times in 776BC (and again in the modern era by Baron Pierre de Coubertin in 1896). It was Heracles who supposedly instituted the custom of rewarding winners with a crown of olive leaves.

Before embarking on either of these adventures, however, the hero underwent another period of servitude, this time to a woman. The punishment came about when he incurred bloodguilt by killing a son of Eurytus, the ruler of the island of Euboea off Greece's eastern coast. Eurytus had insulted Heracles when the hero sought unsuccessfully to wed the king's daughter Iole. Heracles had revenged himself by striking the ruler's son Iphitus down without good cause.

Three Years of Slavery

To make amends, the hero was condemned to serve as a slave for three years. His purchaser was Omphale, Queen of Lydia on the Aegean's eastern coast. She was a beautiful woman, and the hero was soon as much in her thrall emotionally as he was in a legal sense. She enjoyed demonstrating her power over him not merely by getting him to rid her kingdom of robbers and wild beasts but also by persuading him to dress as a woman and sit with her handmaidens spinning.

When the period of this second bondage came to an end, Heracles left Lydia still intent on finding himself a new wife. He finally struck lucky at the court of King Oeneus of Calydon near the mouth of the Gulf of Corinth, where he fell in love with princess Deianira. After fighting a formidable

Women Warriors

Amazon women flouted the Greek natural order, excelling at the traditional male pursuits of hunting and fighting. In some accounts they lopped off their right breasts to make it easier to draw a bow.

Two Amazons corner a Greek. The Amazons worshipped the war god Ares and Artemis, goddess of virginity.

Ruled by a queen, the Amazons lived in an all-woman society. To prevent the race from dying out, they called on the services of a neighbouring people's menfolk once a year, solely for purposes of procreation. Boy children resulting from these brief encounters were sent back to the neighbours, but girls were kept and brought up in the Amazon lands, where they were trained in all the arts of war, learning to fight on horseback armed with battleaxes and bows.

Their homeland was said to be somewhere in Asia Minor, where in historical reality women of the Carian and Phrygian peoples did sometimes bear arms. According to legend, the Amazons founded many cities including the Mediterranean ports of Smyrna and Ephesus, though their realm was usually described as lying on the southern shores of the Black Sea, near modern-day Trabzon. A separate tribe of Libyan Amazons was said to reside on the western borders of Egypt.

rival, the river god Acheloos, he won her hand. Yet it was to be through Deianira that Heracles eventually met his death, although her part in it was unwitting. The true villain of the piece was a centaur named Nessus. One day when the couple were on their way to visit a friend, the centaur offered to carry Deianira over a river, only to run off with her. Heracles at once shot him down with one of the arrows he had tipped with the Hydra's venom (see page 70).

But the dying centaur thought up a cruel way to take his revenge on his killer. Knowing his blood to be poisoned, he instructed Deianira to dip a cloth in it, telling her falsely that it had infallible properties as a love potion; if ever she suspected that she was losing her husband's affections to another woman, he whispered, she must sprinkle some over his clothing and he would never leave her. So saying, Nessus died. Deianira did as he suggested, taking care to hide her

actions from Heracles. They continued on their journey, and when they reached their destination she surreptitiously wrung the blood from the still-damp cloth into a small phial.

Years passed in which she had no need of Nessus's lethal gift, for her husband was too busy for love affairs. He fought battles, sacked cities and challenged champions. Eventually, however, he captured Iole, the princess whose father had refused to have him as a son-in-law.

Appetite for Trouble

Half-man and half-horse, the centaurs had brutish desires that often led to trouble. Yet Chiron, the wisest of them, was revered as a teacher.

As the myths told it, the centaurs were born trouble-makers. They were the progeny of Ixion, a king of the Lapiths, and a cloud-woman created to fool him when he tried to seduce Zeus's consort Hera.

The animal part of their hybrid nature was reflected in their often bestial conduct, especially when they were inflamed with wine. Drunkenness was an element in their celebrated battle with the

Lapith descendants of Ixion (see page 56) as well as in their confrontation with Heracles.

Scholars speculate that stories like these may reflect folk memories of historical clashes with mounted warriors; indeed, the word centaur itself may be related to the Latin *centuria*, meaning a 100-strong war-band. Such warriors were remembered for their prolonged drunken orgies as much as for

Heracles escapes with Iole, princess of Oechalia, after killing her family. The hero had earlier won Iole in an archery contest, but her father refused to hand her over. This Greek marble makes it plain that she was an unwilling prize when he returned to claim her.

Seeing a rival for her husband's affections in her own home, Deianira thought of Nessus's supposed love potion. She had recently prepared a shirt for her husband, and now she rubbed the centaur's blood into it before giving it to him to wear. As the potion began to act, the hero collapsed in agony. Realizing that he was close to death, he gave instructions that he should be taken to a neighbouring peak. It was there, according to a prophecy, that he was destined to die.

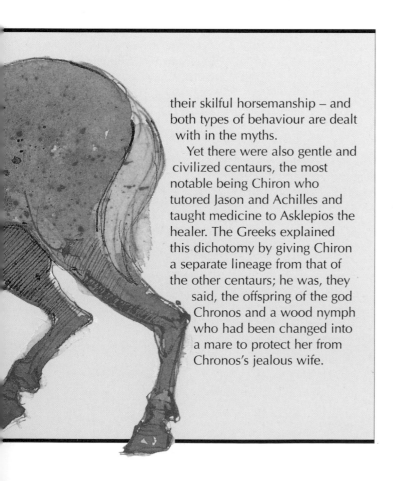

their skilful horsemanship – and both types of behaviour are dealt with in the myths.

Yet there were also gentle and civilized centaurs, the most notable being Chiron who tutored Jason and Achilles and taught medicine to Asklepios the healer. The Greeks explained this dichotomy by giving Chiron a separate lineage from that of the other centaurs; he was, they said, the offspring of the god Chronos and a wood nymph who had been changed into a mare to protect her from Chronos's jealous wife.

The Funeral Pyre of a God

When Heracles reached the mountain summit, his companions informed him that Deianira had taken her own life when she discovered the trick that the centaur had played on her. The hero ordered them to prepare a pyre. When all was ready, he climbed up on to the stack of tinder and gave a command for the fire to be lighted – however, his companions hung back, for none of them dared obey. Finally, a passing shepherd took pity on Heracles's plight and ordered his son Philoctetes to set the pyre alight. In gratitude, Heracles gave the boy his quiver, bow and arrows.

As the flames rose, the bystanders saw the hero reclining serenely on his lionskin, his eyes raised to the heavens. Then a rain of thunderbolts fell from the sky, temporarily blinding them, and when they opened their eyes again both Heracles and the pyre had disappeared. His father Zeus had come to claim him. Heracles's sufferings were over and he had been taken to Mount Olympus to become an immortal and join the gods.

DANGEROUS DAMSELS

The classical myths gave women a greater role in the divine than the human world. The home of the gods, Mount Olympus, was well stocked with assertive females like Hera and Athene who were only too happy to confront and outwit their male counterparts. On Earth, though, the heroic world was an overwhelmingly masculine place in which women most often appeared as damsels in distress, passively awaiting their rescuers. In this male-oriented universe, dominant women generally featured as threatening aberrations: Circe was a scheming enchantress, Jason's wife Medea a child murderer and witch.

Below: A partly gilded bronze by the Renaissance sculptor Pier Giacomo Ilario, known as L'Antico, portrays a downcast Ariadne abandoned by her lover Theseus.

Above: With the licence accorded their status as demi-gods, predatory naiads (water-nymphs) seize the beautiful youth Hylas for their pleasure. This 4th-century AD mosaic is now in Rome's Capitoline Museum.

Above: Few heroines suffered as much as the Trojan princess Cassandra, whose ability to predict the future brought her nothing but pain. Foretelling the fall of Troy, she sought sanctuary in a temple, only to be dragged out and raped, as shown in this Roman wall-painting.

Right: Fated after Troy's fall to become a concubine of the Greek commander Agamemnon, Cassandra was murdered by his wife Clytemnestra when the couple returned to Greece – a scene depicted on this 7th-century BC bronze plaque.

THE TROJAN TRAGEDY

The saga of the siege of Troy has become one of the world's defining myths. In classical times, Homer's account of the conflict in the *Iliad* – the word comes from Ilium, another name for the city of Troy – was regarded not just as the bedrock of Greek literature but also as the beginning of history, taught as fact in every school. Later, when the Renaissance revived interest in the ancient world, the old tales took on a new lease of life, providing writers as diverse as Chaucer, Shakespeare and Racine with inspiration and subject matter for their own works. And even today, whenever people speak of an individual's weak point as an "Achilles heel" or describe someone disgruntled as "sulking in his tent", they are harking back, knowingly or not, to the Western world's oldest and most repeated story.

The tale owes so much to Homer that it is easy to forget that the *Iliad* describes only seven or eight weeks of a siege that lasted ten years. Though it contains references to earlier and later events of the Trojan War, the rest of its history has come down to us mostly from other sources. After the poet's death, a clan of reciters drawn from Homer's circle and collectively known as the *Homeridae* continued his work, and soon a group of half-a-dozen long poems – the so-called Trojan Cycle – had found their way into the repertoire, serving to recount the lead-up to the events of the *Iliad* and the bloody end of the Trojan War. Over the centuries that followed, dozens if not hundreds of Greek and Roman poets added their own gloss to the saga, eliminating inconsistencies, adding picturesque detail, beefing up individual characters, and adding amusing sub-plots.

If later writers returned obsessively to Troy, it was largely because the war became enshrined as the touchstone of past glory. For all its cost in human lives, the siege came to be seen as the measure against which later generations could be tried and found wanting. Homer's near-contemporary Hesiod set the tone when he placed the Homeric protagonists in an Age of Heroes preceding the decadent times in which he thought himself to be living. For, then as now, Achilles and Hector, Odysseus and Helen seemed built to a giant scale, attaining a stature that was somehow more than mortal.

Above: Ancient Greece was a warrior society where the martial arts were an essential part of every boy's education. This 6th-century BC vase shows soldiers running in formation.

Opposite: The father of Chryseis, taken as war booty, begs the Greek leader Agamemnon for her return. This Roman mosaic is in Tunisia.

The Gathering of the Host

The chain of events that led to Troy's destruction began with an intrigue on Mount Olympus. Throughout the long years that followed, the human actors in the tragedy were to be playthings of the gods – their fates determined and their lives destroyed by forces they could never hope to understand.

The wedding procession of the nymph Thetis and the human hero Pelias was as magnificent as it appears on this Etruscan tomb painting from c.570BC. All Olympus was there. But at the feast, the first move was made in the terrible game of the gods that was to climax with the sack of Troy.

Among the beauties who stirred Zeus's fancy was the sea-nymph Thetis. He would no doubt have forced his attentions on her but for a prophecy that Thetis's son would grow up greater than his father. So the chief of the gods abandoned the idea of a liaison with the nymph and decided to find a safe husband for her. He selected a human hero, Peleus, who had sailed with the *Argo*.

Thetis herself was less than pleased to become the bride of a mortal. Only when Zeus guaranteed her a grand wedding with all Olympus in attendance did she consent to become betrothed. Zeus lived up to his word, and the day was everything Thetis could have wished. But among the company, there was one uninvited guest, Eris – "Strife". Yet she turned up anyway, intent on revenging herself for the slight.

Bursting into the feast, she tossed an apple bearing the inscription "For the Fairest" on to the table where the principal goddesses sat. Three deities at once claimed the fruit: Zeus's consort Hera; his daughter Athene, goddess of wisdom; and Aphrodite, the radiant divinity of beauty and love. The trio appealed to Zeus to settle the dispute. But he, realizing the jealousies any judgement would stir up, decided to delegate the task.

The judge he chose was Paris, a mortal who was then earning his living as a cowherd on Mount Ida. He had attracted the attention of the gods first by boasting that his herd included the finest bull in the region; and then, when the god Ares jestingly took on a bull's form to contest the claim, by unhesitatingly admitting the challenger's supremacy. This act won him a reputation for fairness.

When Zeus's messenger Hermes brought Paris to make the judgement, each contender did her best to influence his choice. Hera offered him power over men and nations; Athene promised the gift of wisdom and good counsel. But Paris had eyes only for Aphrodite who, as goddess of love, promised him the most beautiful woman in the world. As Paris gave her the apple, she curled her lip in triumph; but her two defeated rivals made no attempt to conceal their bitterness.

Their hatred was to have momentous consequences, for Paris, as it happened, was no ordinary cowherd. He had been born a son of Priam, king of Troy, but at his birth a prophet had foretold that he would cause the ruin of the city, so his father had decided that the baby must be left to die on the flanks of Mount Ida. But little Paris was saved first by a she-bear who suckled him, and then by a servant of Priam who took the infant into his own household and brought him up to herd cattle.

Paris grew to be a youth of great strength and beauty. Not long after his trip to Olympus, messengers from King Priam came to Ida seeking a bull to sacrifice at games that were to take place in the city. Paris decided to compete, and returned to Troy with the envoys. He won all the contests he entered, drawing so much attention to himself that the retainer who had sheltered him came forward to reveal that the young man was Priam's son. The king was so impressed by Paris's feats that, dismissing earlier fears, he restored his son to the palace.

And so it was as a prince of Troy that Paris claimed his prize from Aphrodite; and the goddess revealed to him that it took the glorious shape of Helen, Queen of Sparta, and daughter of Zeus. Unfortunately, she was also the wife of Menelaus. Helen was the result of Zeus's liaison with Leda, wife of the Spartan king Tyndareus. As Helen grew up, the fame of her loveliness spread, and when she reached marriageable age she was courted by most of the leading figures in the Greek world. Indeed, she had so many influential suitors that Tyndareus became worried that those she rejected might turn sour. So, on the advice of the cunning Odysseus, he got all the contenders to swear to come to the aid of her future husband if anyone should challenge his

Menelaus, Helen's husband, inherited the kingdom of Sparta on the Peloponnese from his wife's stepfather, King Tyndareus. Menelaus's brother, Agamemnon, the king of neighbouring Mycenae, was married to Helen's sister, Clytemnestra. Together, Sparta and Mycenae were the leading powers on mainland Greece. This sculpture shows Menelaus ready for battle.

position. Eventually Helen chose the handsome and aristocratic Menelaus as her husband and her stepfather made him King of Sparta.

The Abduction of Helen

When Paris arrived at Sparta with a fleet from Troy, Menelaus received the Trojan prince as an honoured guest. Paris repaid his hospitality by seducing his wife, a task that, with Aphrodite's aid, he soon accomplished. So when Menelaus was called away to Crete, Paris had little trouble in persuading Helen to flee with him to Troy.

When the Spartan king came home to find his wife gone, he turned first to his brother, Greece's most powerful king, Agamemnon of Mycenae. Then he called on all Helen's old suitors. Agamemnon sent envoys to King Priam in Troy to demand restitution; but when they returned empty-handed, the Mycenaean ruler sent out a general call to arms.

Some of Helen's former suitors proved less than eager to respond. Odysseus, who was by then happily married, pretended to be mad. Envoys found him dressed in peasant's clothing ploughing the beach, throwing salt over his shoulder as he went as if it were seed. When he pretended not to recognize his distinguished guests, a wily nobleman named Palamedes seized Odysseus's infant son and threw him in the path of the plough. At once the supposed madman rushed to the boy's rescue. Unmasked, Odysseus sheepishly agreed to join Agamemnon's army; but he harboured a lasting grudge against Palamedes.

Eventually all the forces gathered at the port of Aulis on Greece's Aegean coast, where they were bolstered by a sizeable contingent from Crete

Early listeners to Homer's epic of Troy would have imagined the heroes wearing armour such as this 6th-century BC bronze helmet.

under Idomeneus, the island's king. Among the others who answered the call was the brave warrior Diomedes, who had been deeply in love with Helen, and wise old Nestor, the king of Pylus, whose counsel was prized above all others'. There was Ajax, a giant of a man and a feared fighter, and Calchas, a renegade from Troy whose gift of prophecy had suggested to him that he might be better off supporting Greece than Troy. But no warrior was more eagerly welcomed than the mighty Achilles, who arrived in the company of his cousin and closest friend, Patroclus.

Before the fleet set sail, a strange event took place that was considered a portent. As Agamemnon was sacrificing to Zeus, a snake darted from beneath the altar and up a tree. There it devoured eight fledgling sparrows in a nest, finally swallowing the mother bird. Immediately it froze into immobility and turned to stone. Calchas at once recognized a sign from Zeus: the coming war would continue through eight years, but in the ninth would reach a successful conclusion. Cheered by the omen, the army set sail.

But they had no pilot to guide them, and they struck the Asian coast not on Trojan soil but at neighbouring Mysia. Seeing his realm invaded, its king Telephus led his troops out to do battle. The fight that followed was short but sharp; the Greeks suffered their first casualties, and Telephus himself was wounded by Achilles, who speared him in the thigh. Then, realizing their mistake, Agamemnon's men returned to their ships and sailed back to the Greek mainland.

Telephus's wound festered and refused to mend. He sent envoys to the oracle at Delphi in search of a cure, and they came back with the pronouncement that only the giver of the wound could heal it. So Telephus took ship across the Aegean and, disguising himself as a beggar, made his way into the Greek camp. There he seized Agamemnon's infant son, Orestes, threatening to kill the baby unless Achilles cured him. But Odysseus, on hearing the oracle, suggested that the words might apply to the weapon rather than the man. Sure enough, a scraping of rust from Achilles's spear did the trick when applied to Telephus's thigh; and in return, the Mysian king agreed to give the fleet directions to Troy.

The Goddess Demands a Sacrifice

So the great host gathered once more at Aulis for the expedition to begin. But they were thwarted again, for this time no wind sprang up to carry them eastward across the Aegean. As days of forced inactivity turned to weeks, the Greek leaders turned to Calchas for an explanation. Agamemnon had angered Artemis, the seer proclaimed, by boasting that he was more skilled in the hunt than she was. She would only send a favourable wind if the king propitiated her by offering up Iphigenia, the most beautiful of his daughters, as a sacrifice to the goddess. When Agamemnon first heard Calchas's suggestion, he indignantly refused to consider the idea. But as time passed and his forces became increasingly restless, he had second thoughts. Eventually he sent messengers to Sparta to seek the young girl; and to calm his wife Clytemnestra's fears, he instructed them to spread the word that he intended Iphigenia to be the bride of Achilles.

Delighted by the news, the happy mother accompanied her daughter to the camp, but on meeting Achilles she learned of her husband's deception. Frantically she begged him to spare the girl, but Agamemnon's mind was made up. And so Iphigenia had to give up her life for her father's cause; though some say that at the last moment Artemis herself relented (see box, page 87).

Soon the winds set fair for Troy, and the fleet set off once more. Landing on Tenedos, within sight of their destination, they quickly took control

Greek soldiers had little protection aside from their elaborate plumed helmets and light, round shields. Horses would have been a luxury available only to the wealthy.

When they reached Troy, the Greeks set up camp, ready for the long siege that had been predicted by the prophet Calchas. This red-figure vase from *c.*490BC shows their temporary dwelling.

to leave the boats, for they had heard a prophecy that the first man to do so would be the first to die. Eventually Protesilaus, an uncle of Philoctetes, leaped into the surf and, shouting a war cry, charged the Trojan forces drawn up on the beach. He killed several men before he was cut down by Hector; but by that time the rest of Agamemnon's army had followed his example, and they soon drove the foe back to the walls of their city a few kilometres away across the coastal plain.

Having established a beach-head, the Greeks drew their ships up behind a stockade and settled down for a lengthy campaign. Even though their fleet numbered a thousand vessels, they had neither the men nor the resources to invest the town, so throughout the long years of war the Trojans were able to replenish their stocks of food and to receive reinforcements freely. Agamemnon, therefore, launched a war of attrition. The Greeks concentrated on attacking and sacking the smaller towns of the Troad, ravaging the surrounding countryside, and staging raids on Troy's many allies along the coast and on nearby islands.

of the island, killing its ruler in the fray. In the course of the celebration that followed, a snake bit the famous archer Philoctetes in the foot. The wound turned septic, causing him agonizing pain, and his constant groans so disturbed his comrades that Agamemnon's patience snapped. He ordered Odysseus to take the archer to the nearby island of Lemnos and maroon him. The castaway was to survive there for many years, living on what he could forage in the wild; and in time his comrades would have need of him again.

A strait only ten kilometres wide separated the Greek army at Tenedos from the Troad, as the region around Troy was known. But before launching their attack, the invaders made a final attempt to reclaim Helen peacefully. Menelaus, Odysseus and Palamedes went to the city to demand the return of Helen. But by this time the Trojans had made up their minds, and they sent the envoys back empty-handed. Some even wished to kill them; but Antenor, a leading citizen in whose house they were staying, insisted that no harm should be done to his guests.

The Greeks then lost no more time in landing on enemy soil. Yet their warriors initially hesitated

Odysseus's Revenge

Few details survive of the first years of the war, but one story tells of the unsavoury revenge of Odysseus on Palamedes, who had exposed his feigned madness. The Ithacan ruler forced a prisoner to forge a letter, purportedly from King Priam, promising Palamedes payment in return for betraying the Greek camp. When his tent was subsequently searched, gold was indeed found buried beneath it – where it had been placed shortly before on Odysseus's orders. This act of underhand cunning proved lethally effective. Palamedes vehemently protested his innocence, but he was put on trial for treason, found guilty and stoned to death. This incident illustrates one of the Troy saga's distinctive features: its harsh moral realism.

Iphigenia's Escape

The sacrifice of Iphigenia to Artemis to secure favourable winds for Agamemnon's fleet shocked the Greeks. So poets put forward an alternative version with a happy ending, in which the goddess herself intervened to save the young princess.

According to the happy version, Artemis appeared in person as the young girl was stretched out beneath the sacrificial knife and snatched her away to safety, leaving a hind to be killed in her place. The goddess carried her to the land of the Tauroi, who lived far away across the Black Sea in what is now the Crimea. There the Greek princess became a priestess in a temple that contained a celebrated image of the goddess.

It was the custom of this barbarous land to sacrifice to Artemis all strangers who visited the country, and for many years Iphigenia was forced to preside over these bloody rites. Then one day her own brother Orestes came to Taurian shores and was handed over to her to be killed.

Recognizing one another, the long-separated pair suppressed their joy at the unexpected reunion only long enough to plan their escape. And when they did succeed in slipping away, they took the statue of Artemis with them to find a more suitable home for it in Greece. In later years, many cities claimed to be the statue's final resting place. At home, Iphigenia became a priestess to Artemis again.

JUDGEMENT OF PARIS

Over the centuries, the classical myths have attracted the attention of artists of many nations, and few episodes in them have proved more popular than the Judgement of Paris. The story tells how the young Trojan prince of that name was summoned from guarding flocks on Mount Ida to adjudicate a divine beauty contest. He awarded the prize to Aphrodite, providing painters of all eras with the chance to depict the charms of the Goddess of Love herself alongside those of her defeated rivals Athene and Hera.

Though different in style, two versions of the myth painted 350 years apart share common features. The 16th-century Swiss artist Niklaus Manuel depicts a clothed and bearded Paris (top), while the 19th-century French symbolist Elie Delaunay shows him naked (left). Both artists delight in rendering ideals of female beauty.

Below: Hermes leads the three goddesses to a pastoral judgement seat in a fresco by the Renaissance master Giulio Romano from the Palazzo Ducale in Mantua.

Bottom: Rubens's lush and fleshy *Judgement of Paris* identifies Hera by her peacock and Athene by her shield, adorned with the head of the Gorgon Medusa, whom she had helped Perseus to kill.

The Wrath of Achilles

The segment of the Troy saga described in Homer's *Iliad* covers only a brief period in the ninth and final year of the war. But it is a decisive moment when the military stand-off comes to an end, and the opposing forces meet in open battle, face to face.

Homer himself accurately described the subject of his epic in its opening lines, when he calls on the Muse to sing "the wrath of Achilles". The 15,692 lines that follow recount the hero's quarrel with Agamemnon, the supreme commander of the Greek forces, and its dire consequences for all concerned. The action plays out on two levels: in the human sphere, where men fight and die horribly in hand-to-hand combat on the battlefield; and among the Immortals, who loftily and unconcernedly manipulate the fate of the human players in an unending struggle for status.

Just as the entire war was fought over the lovely Helen, so Agamemnon and Achilles fell out over a woman. Her name was Briseis, and she had been seized as booty in the course of one of the many minor actions that took up the first eight years of the siege. She was assigned as a concubine to Achilles, who cherished her for her beauty.

Meanwhile Agamemnon had acquired a mistress of his own in similar fashion. Called Chryseis, she was the daughter of a priest of Apollo in one of the cities of the Troad that the Greeks had stormed. When her father tried to ransom her, the Mycenaean ruler scornfully rejected his offer. The priest then prayed to Apollo, who heard his prayer. To punish Agamemnon's arrogance, he sent a plague to afflict the Greek ranks. Soon the camp was loud with the cries of the sick and dying.

A Bitter Dispute

The seer Calchas revealed that Apollo must be appeased if the scourge was to be lifted, and Agamemnon angrily agreed to send Chryseis back. But he demanded compensation for his sacrifice – and he chose to take it in the form of Briseis.

This Etruscan fresco depicts the mounted warrior Achilles waiting outside the walls of Troy. In the ancient world, Achilles was considered the epitome of manly courage.

When Achilles was informed that he was to lose the girl, he flew into a rage. As commander-in-chief of the expedition, Agamemnon apportioned all booty, human or otherwise, that was seized in the course of the campaigns, and he was technically within his rights in demanding Briseis.

Achilles was forced to swallow his pride and consent to his commander's bidding. However, to show his bitter resentment, he retreated to his tent and swore loudly that he and the force he commanded, the much-feared Myrmidons of Thessaly, would play no further part in the war. In his anger,

The Childhood of Achilles

Fearing what the future might have in store for her warrior son, Thetis did all she could to shield him from danger. But destiny decreed that all her efforts were to be in vain.

In this Roman fresco of Achilles on Skyros, Odysseus (top right) has arrived to take the young hero to war.

Forced by Zeus to marry a mortal (see page 82), Thetis vowed that no child of hers should bear her husband's taint. So she cast her first six offspring into fire, hoping to burn all that was not divine out of them. None survived. But when a seventh baby was born, her husband Peleus stopped her, saving the infant's life.

The boy grew up strong and handsome, and Thetis soon became reconciled to him, naming him Achilles. Yet, still fearing his human weakness, she made one more attempt to protect him. Taking him to the Styx, the Underworld river whose waters were believed to convey immortality, she dipped him in. His whole body was submerged but for the heel by which she held him – and that was to remain fatally vulnerable.

For his education, Achilles was sent to an unlikely tutor. Chiron was a centaur who lived on remote Mount Pelion; but he was renowned for his wisdom. Under his tutelage the young man grew up unmatched in the arts of peace and war.

So when news came that all the greatest warriors of Greece were gathering to attack Troy, Thetis at once feared that her son would be summoned. To protect him, she disguised him as a girl and sent him to the island of Skyros. The king's daughter Deidameia was only too happy to learn the truth of the imposture; in time she bore the newcomer a son.

Yet, as Thetis had feared, envoys eventually tracked Achilles down. At first they had difficulty distinguishing him, for his real identity was well hidden. But then wily Odysseus employed a clever ruse. He sent a selection of gifts into the women's quarters that included, alongside jewellery and personal adornments, some armour and a sword. When one of the maidens was subsequently seen practising swordplay, the envoys at once recognized their target, Achilles. At their demand he consented to set off to the war, thereby realizing all his doting mother's worst fears.

Achilles turned for help to his mother Thetis. She took his case to Zeus, who agreed to give the Trojans the upper hand in the struggle until the slight had been avenged. To that end, the god sent a deceitful dream to Agamemnon, seeming to promise the Greek king victory if he led out his forces for a pitched battle.

When the opposing armies confronted each other, the Trojan leader Hector strode forward with a proposition. Since it was the quarrel of Paris and Menelaus over Helen that had caused the war, he suggested, let the two men settle their difference in single combat. Both armies welcomed the suggestion, and a truce was hastily arranged to allow the fight to take place.

Heroes in Single Combat

The two champions, Paris and Menelaus, confronted one another in the no- man's- land between the Greek and Trojan armies. Menelaus had the better of the fight and was on the point of killing Paris, a deed that might have allowed him to reclaim Helen and bring the long war to an end. But divine intervention quickly scuppered that possibility. First Aphrodite, seeing her beloved Paris close to death, chose to wrap him in a mist and waft him away from the battle to the safety of the bed chamber that he shared with Helen. Then Athene, bent on Troy's destruction, induced a Trojan, Pandarus, to loose an arrow at Menelaus, wounding him slightly in the thigh. This sudden and treacherous attack at once broke the truce, and all chance of a peaceful conclusion to the struggle was definitely at an end.

The Greeks fought bravely in the ensuing fray, fired up by anger at the Trojan's perfidy. Diomedes in particular raged through the enemy ranks, first wounding Aeneas and then nicking Aphrodite herself in the wrist when she rushed to carry the young prince to safety. Even Ares, god of war, was not immune; when he came down to rally the Trojan ranks, a Greek warrior speared him in the loins, sending him post-haste back to his home on Mount Olympus. Even so, the battle

remained indecisive, and the Greeks had eventually to withdraw to their camp and to strengthen its fortifications against a possible Trojan attack.

The warlords met in conclave, and Agamemnon allowed himself to be persuaded that they could not hope to win the war without Achilles's assistance. He sent heralds and emissaries – led by Odysseus – to the sulking warrior, offering lavish amends for the affront earlier offered him. Agamemnon promised not only to return the beautiful Briseis untouched, along with lavish gifts of horses, gold and slaves; he also offered Achilles the choice of his own royal daughters for a wife when the expedition eventually returned to Greece, along with a dowry of seven cities.

The proposition was a generous one, and the envoys were startled when Achilles turned it down, saying that he planned to set sail for home on the following morning and reiterating that he would only consent to fight when his own ships were threatened. This was a major setback to the Greek cause and Agamemnon, disheartened, began to plan a withdrawal.

A Stealthy Night Attack

At this time of crisis, Odysseus showed greater fortitude. He decided to take advantage of the fact that the Trojan army was bivouacked outside the walls of the city to stage a guerrilla raid. Taking Diomedes as a companion, he infiltrated the Trojan lines by moonlight.

The two Greeks killed a patrolling guard after forcing him to reveal details of the layout of the Trojan encampment. Then, armed with this information, they found their way to the tent of King Rhesus, who had arrived that very day with reinforcements from Thrace. They killed the slumbering ruler and his twelve companions, then drove his magnificent white horses back to the Greek lines – an important prize, for it had been prophesied that Troy would never fall if these beasts drank from the nearby River Scamander.

Despite this small victory, the next day went badly for Agamemnon's men. Hector led the

Trojan forces like a man possessed, and one by one all the Greek champions – Odysseus, Diomedes, even the king – were worsted and wounded in the fighting. For a while Poseidon lent his aid to the Greeks, helping to keep the Trojans at bay. During this stage of the fighting, Ajax almost succeeded in crushing Hector with a heavy rock. But Zeus ordered the sea god from the battlefield, restored Hector's strength and fired up the

Trojans' valour. The attackers swept forward once more. Then the line of defences protecting the Greek ships was breached. One of the vessels was set alight and the flames blazed in the sky.

The Two Armies

Both sides in the Trojan conflict had their share of heroes. Below are the most famous.

THE GREEKS
Achilles the Greeks' greatest warrior
Agamemnon king of Mycenae and leader of the Greek forces
Ajax the best fighter after Achilles
The lesser Ajax a warrior who was to anger the gods by raping Priam's daughter Cassandra
Calchas Trojan seer who defected to the Greek camp and forecast Achilles's role in Troy's fall
Diomedes A fine warrior and Odysseus's trusted companion on several forays
Menelaus king of Sparta, husband of Helen and brother of Agamemnon
Nestor king of Pylos, respected for his wisdom
Odysseus a cunning and wily fighter
Patroclus Achilles's cousin and best friend

THE TROJANS AND THEIR ALLIES
Aeneas a son of Aphrodite who would go on to have his own legend
Glaucus Troy's Lycian ally
Hector King Priam's eldest son and the Trojans' finest warrior
Paris another of Priam's sons, Helen's seducer and so provoker of the Trojan War
Priam king of Troy
Penthesilea queen of the Amazons
Memnon king of Ethiopia and the most handsome man alive
Rhesus king of Thrace and owner of a magnificent team of horses

Patroclus Pleads with his Cousin

In this desperate situation, Achilles's beloved cousin Patroclus appealed once more to the Greek champion to forget his grievance and join the battle against the Trojans. Achilles again would not agree to fight in person, but this time relented sufficiently to allow Patroclus to lead out the Myrmidons in his place. In addition, Achilles lent his cousin his own magnificent armour, knowing that merely the sight of it would spread terror through the Trojan ranks, like flames through dry wood. However, he also gave Patroclus strict instructions only to drive the Trojans back from the Greek ships and not to follow the enemy as they retreated back to the walls of Troy itself.

The ruse worked. At the sight of Achilles's armour the Greeks took heart and the Trojans fell back. Buoyed by his reflected glory, Patroclus fought as he had never before, slaying Sarpedon, a son of Zeus and commander of the Lycian contingent, and driving the enemy back towards Troy. In the heat of battle he forgot Achilles's warning and pursued the foe to the walls of the city. There the god Apollo, hidden in a cloud of mist, struck him down, knocking his shield and weapons away and rendering him powerless; and Hector, seizing the opportunity, delivered the coup de grace. Then in his triumph he stripped off Achilles's armour as a battle trophy; and it was with great difficulty that the Greeks managed to rescue Patroclus's body from Trojan hands.

When Achilles heard the news of his friend's death, he was seized by a paroxysm of grief, tearing his hair and strewing dust clawed from the ground over his face. Then, furious for revenge, he rushed unarmed to the ramparts and let out a terrible battle-cry. The sight of the hero Achilles and the blood-curdling howl he emitted were so fearsome that the Trojans stopped in their tracks.

The Greeks took advantage of this respite to drag Patroclus's battered, lifeless body back behind the safety of their own lines.

The Vengeance of Achilles

Equipped with brand new armour made for him by the god Hephaistos (see box page 96), Achilles rose the next day with only one thought in his head: revenge on Hector for the killing of his friend. Even a warning from his mother Thetis that his own death would soon follow that of the Trojan champion could not restrain Achilles. Before setting out to seek his adversary, however, he first made his peace with Agamemnon, accepting the offer the envoys had brought him a couple of days earlier and taking Briseis back again.

Then Achilles went to war. No Trojan dared face the Greek hero in his battle fury, and the enemy army broke and fled before him towards the River Scamander. The river god himself rose against the Greek, only to be beaten back – in some accounts, Hephaistos directed a blaze of flame at the river, drying it up in an instant. As for Achilles's human foes, those who survived the onslaught fled back to the safety of the city like a pack of frightened animals.

Only Hector was brave enough to face Achilles. He waited alone outside the gates of Troy to meet the Greek. But even the most gallant of the

Clean-shaven Achilles lunges forward to kill the already bleeding Hector in this scene from an Attic vase. The heroes fight with long lances leaving their swords sheathed.

Trojans was unnerved by the sight of the fearsome warrior with the light flashing off his bronze armour like the sun itself, and for all his good intentions Hector took to his heels. Some sources say he hoped to tire the Greek, knowing that Achilles had been inactive for some time and was therefore not as fit as usual.

Three times Achilles chased him round the walls of Troy while Hector's fellow citizens looked on in horror from the ramparts. Each time he tried to take shelter at one of the gates, Achilles drove him back into the open. Then the goddess Athene granted the Trojan a fresh access of courage, and he turned on his pursuer for what he knew would be a last stand. He fought bravely but his fears were soon realized, for Achilles quickly killed him with a spear thrust through the throat.

With his dying breath, Hector beseeched Achilles to treat his body with respect, reminding him of his own impending doom. But the Greek champion's anger was still undimmed. Stripping the corpse of the defeated Hector, he tied it to his chariot and dragged it unceremoniously away feet-first. Hector's long black hair spread out behind him as his head bumped across the hard ground. A great cloud of dust rose up behind Achilles as he

Troy's Tragic Champion

To modern eyes, the Iliad's supreme military champion Achilles seems a self-absorbed killing machine, as obsessed with his own image as any of the Olympians. The Trojan Hector now appears the more attractive figure, showing genuine concern over his family's and his country's fate.

As Priam's eldest son and heir, Hector was the leader of the Trojan forces and a born warrior. Yet as Homer presents the story, military honour was not his only concern. Because of his awareness of the damage war could do, it was he who proposed that Menelaus and Paris should settle their quarrel in single combat, so obviating the need for further bloodshed.

When his peace-making efforts came to nothing, Hector resigned himself to seeing through a contest that he sensed could only lead to disaster. He led the Trojan forces bravely, driving the Greek invaders back to their ships and taking on Achilles's friend Patroclus hand-to-hand. By killing Patroclus he became the target of Achilles's murderous wrath, eventually meeting at the Greek hero's hands the death fated on him by the implacable hatred of the goddess Athene, the deadly foe of Troy.

Two scenes in the *Iliad* add a note of pathos to his death. One is his leave-taking of his wife Andromache and their young son. When the warrior tries to kiss the boy farewell, the child instinctively shies back, terrified by his father's bronze helmet with its crest of horsehair bristles. Laughing, the proud father lifts it off to show his face and then clasps his son in a final embrace.

The other is the hero's one recorded moment of weakness. When Achilles confronts him in his battle-frenzy, the champion's nerve suddenly cracks and he flees from his adversary, who chases him three times round the walls of Troy. Then Hector finds fresh courage to confront his pursuer, going with dignity to the death he knows must follow. Such moments of fallibility, unknown to his mighty adversary, may not have enhanced his military reputation, but they give him a human dimension that his more single-minded opponent signally lacks.

dragged his terrible booty back to the Greek camp. Once he had returned, his thoughts turned again to Patroclus, and to the need to give his friend a fitting burial. On his cousin's pyre, built of wood from Mount Ida, Achilles sacrificed not just horses and two of his friend's loyal hounds but also a dozen nobly born Trojan prisoners-of-war, some of them sons of King Priam himself.

Overcome once again with emotion, he was about to hurl Hector's corpse to the surviving hounds of Patroclus's pack, when the goddess Aphrodite intervened and persuaded him to refrain from this brutal act. After the immolation, Achilles set about organizing funeral games in which all the Greek commanders took part; Diomedes won the chariot race, while Odysseus and Ajax were jointly awarded the crown for wrestling.

Meanwhile, Achilles continued to treat the Trojan's body with hatred and contempt, attaching it to his chariot again each morning to drag it round Patroclus's pyre. Eventually the gods, who had miraculously preserved the corpse from

The Armour of Achilles

Courage, strength and fighting spirit were the key qualities of the Homeric hero. But the Iliad *also pays due regard to the arms the warriors bore – and none had a panoply to match the one Hephaistos, god of metal-working, made for Achilles.*

When Hector killed Patroclus, he stripped the armour Achilles had lent the dead warrior off the body. Mad for revenge, the Greek champion had to delay his retaliation until his mother, the sea-nymph Thetis, could get him new equipment from the divine smith Hephaistos.

The *Iliad* describes in loving detail the armour that the god made. First there was a breastplate, glowing brighter than fire, then flexible tin greaves to guard the legs against sword cuts. A gold-crested helmet sheathed the head and face. But Homer reserves most of his eloquence for the shield, on which Hephaistos engraved images of a microcosm of the entire Greek world – scenes of agriculture, husbandry, warfare, celebration and counsel, all rimmed by the mighty River Ocean then thought to encircle the earth.

In highlighting the armour, Homer was only reflecting historical Bronze Age realities. At the time, metal was an expensive luxury only available to an elite of warrior aristocrats. The competitive edge their arms gave them on the battlefield ensured their superiority over other combatants, thus providing the technological underpinning upon which the Age of Heroes was based.

The god Hephaistos, Aphrodite's oft-cuckolded husband, was the Olympian blacksmith, so the armour he made for Achilles was the best in the world. The Romans identified Hephaistos with their fire god, Vulcan, shown here in a leather smith's hat.

mutilation and decay, decided that enough was enough: Achilles vengeance was complete. At a divine council on Mount Olympus, they determined that the remains should be returned to Troy, so that Hector could be properly laid to rest. Thetis was dispatched to inform Achilles, while the goddess Iris sped to Priam's palace to tell him to prepare a suitable ransom for the dead hero.

On Zeus's orders, Hermes accompanied the Trojan king to his sad tryst, ensuring him safe conduct to the tent of Achilles. The Trojan queen, Hecuba, had warned her husband to expect no mercy from the man who had killed so many of their sons, but the old warrior's grief struck a chord with Achilles, reminding him of his feelings for his own father, Peleus.

With sorrow but no hint of bitterness, the old king pleaded for the return of Hector's body. His directness touched Achilles, who now for the first time since the death of Hector showed stirrings of pity. The two enemies mourned their dead together, and Achilles promised to arrange a twelve-day truce to allow King Priam time to organize a suitable funeral.

Hermes saw the king safely back to Troy with his blood-stained burden. And there, in Troy, Hector's body was finally burned atop a mighty funeral pyre, and the charred bones set in a golden chest buried beneath a mound of stones. The *Iliad* comes to an end with the words: "And so the Trojans buried Hector, breaker of horses."

Old King Priam falls on bended knee to beg the hot-headed young warrior Achilles for the body of his son on this silver-gilt Roman drinking vessel. Achilles had shown little respect for Hector's corpse previously, so Priam has no reason to hope for mercy, but as the king's age and bearing remind Achilles of his own much-loved father, he begins to soften.

The Fall of Troy

With the death of Hector, the Trojans had lost their greatest champion. Yet their Greek assailants still had to overcome many other hurdles before they could finally attain their goal; and even then the long-sought-for victory brought them little happiness.

After eight years of war, the defenders of Troy could feel the Greek noose tightening around them. The countryside around the city had been devastated, and most of the lesser towns of the Troad sacked. Yet allies still rallied to their defence, among them Queen Penthesilea's Amazons (see box, page 75).

Another exotic force that came to help their cause were the Ethiopians of King Memnon. He was the son of the dawn goddess Eos, a fine fighter and reputedly the most handsome man alive. Taking the field against the Greeks, he killed many warriors including Nestor's son Antilochus, who was struck down trying to protect his father. Eventually he agreed to meet Ajax in single combat; but Achilles, learning of Antilochus's death, insisted on taking on the African champion himself and duly killed him, throwing his head and armour on to the young Greek's funeral pyre.

The Death of Achilles

Yet Achilles's own end was now near. As he pursued the fleeing Trojans back to the city, Paris loosed an arrow at him. The god Apollo himself guided the shaft, and the poisoned tip struck the Greek in the heel, the only part of his body where he was vulnerable. With a terrible cry, Achilles died; and for a few moments the fighting came to a halt as news of the champion's death spread through the ranks. Then the Trojans rushed to seize his corpse, and for hours battle raged around it. Finally Ajax succeeded in carrying it back to the Greek camp, where it was burned with honour.

The Greeks held funeral games for Achilles just as he himself had done for Patroclus, and in their course Agamemnon, at Thetis's suggestion,

made the rash promise that the dead man's wonderful armour should be given to the warrior who most deserved it. Odysseus and Ajax both claimed the honour, and for long the Greek leaders argued in council over which of the two had the better claim. Eventually they decided to settle the matter by sending spies to listen under the walls of Troy. The prize would go to whichever of the two their enemies most feared.

When the answer came back in Odysseus's favour, Ajax went mad with rage and grief. He stormed out of his tent that night intending to kill the Greek chiefs who had insulted him; but the goddess Athene was watching, and she led him astray into the animal enclosures, where he only killed sheep and cattle. Coming to his senses again the following morning, he was so ashamed of his actions that he went to a secluded spot outside the camp and fell on his sword, killing himself.

Stunned by the loss of two of their champions in so short a time, the Greeks sought reasons for their misfortunes. They had been promised that Troy would fall after nine years of fighting, but they were now well into the ninth and still seemed to be making little headway. In their bewilderment, they turned once more to Calchas, who said Troy could only be taken with the aid of Heracles's bow and arrows, which alone could kill Paris. But these were in the possession of Philoctetes, abandoned so long ago on the isle of Lemnos.

Odysseus was dispatched with Diomedes to track down the castaway. Amazingly, they found him alive, a filthy and bedraggled figure with his wound still festering. Odysseus realized that this living scarecrow had no reason to do the Greeks any favours, and so resorted to his usual cunning to trick him out of the weapons.

Achilles kills the Amazon queen in this red-figure vase from *c.*540BC. Achilles stabbed her through the heart with his spear. Then, as the queen's dying body fell to the ground, her helmet fell off her head and her long hair tumbled free. Achilles, seeing how beautiful she was, fell in love with her and protected her body from being desecrated by the Greeks.

Diomedes, however, insisted on appealing to his better nature, asking him to come to the Greek camp of his own free will. Philoctetes might well have demurred had not Heracles himself – now a god – appeared to him, telling him to go and informing him too of another precondition for the fall of Troy: that Achilles's son, Neoptolemus, should join the Greek forces. So the three men travelled on to Skyros, where Odysseus persuaded the young warrior to go to the war despite the pleas of his despairing mother Deidameia.

Back in the Greek camp, Philoctetes finally had his wound cured by the surgeon Machaon. Then, taking up Heracles's bow, he ventured forth to challenge Paris. His first arrow went wide, but the second and third found their mark, fatally wounding the Trojan.

Helenus's Revenge

The Greeks were further encouraged by a tip from a captive Trojan. This warrior, Helenus, had hoped to marry Helen after Paris's death. When she was given to his brother Deiphobus instead, he got his own back by revealing a secret vital to Troy's survival: his countrymen fought in the certainty that their city could never fall so long as it was under the protection of the Palladium, or Luck of Troy – an image of Pallas Athene said to have been cast down from heaven by the goddess herself.

The Greeks decided then and there that the statue would have to be stolen, and once more Odysseus volunteered. As a preliminary, he decided to go on a reconnaissance mission to find out how the image could best be removed. To gain admittance to Troy, he disguised himself as a beggar and had himself beaten by his comrades until blood ran. He presented himself at the city's gates, claiming to come as a fugitive from the Greeks.

The guards, thinking that he might be able to provide information on the Greek camp, allowed him into the city. He remained inside the enemy's walls for some hours, undetected save by one person: Helen herself. She drew him aside surreptitiously to let him know that ever since Paris's death she had been held in Troy against her will, and to promise the Greeks all assistance she could give them in taking the city.

Eventually Odysseus slipped back to the Greek lines, where he laid plans to return with Diomedes under cover of darkness to snatch the Palladium. The two gained admittance to the city through a drain that Odysseus had located on his earlier visit, and between them they managed to remove the statue from its temple home. Carrying it stealthily through the sleeping streets, they exited as they had entered and regained their camp. Fearing to arouse the goddess's anger by displaying their trophy, they hid it on Mount Ida.

The success of this venture set Odysseus's mind working for other ways to smuggle soldiers into Troy. The drain could not be used again, for the Trojans would have traced his footsteps to it. But he felt sure that there must be some other stratagem that could be used to penetrate the city's formidable defences. And before long he had it.

At his suggestion, carpenters used timber from Mount Ida to make a gigantic wooden horse. It was set on wheels so that it could be easily moved, and inside it was left hollow. In the belly of the beast a door that could only be opened by an internal catch was cunningly concealed. Within the horse's flanks there was room for thirty fully armed warriors to lie concealed in darkness.

The next problem was to get the horse into Troy, and to this end Odysseus employed all his celebrated wits. He persuaded Agamemnon to break camp overnight and withdraw with all his ships, so that the Trojans would think the Greeks had finally abandoned the siege. In fact, the fleet only sailed as far as the offshore island of Tenedos, taking shelter on its lee side only a few kilometres from the point of departure.

Troy's citizens carried on unaware of the terrible fate which was soon to befall them. They did not heed the warnings of the princess Cassandra, who told them that their doom was imminent. The princess had the gift of prophecy, going into a trance before she spoke. But the people of the city believed she was mad.

Prophetess of Doom

The most tragic of King Priam's twelve daughters was the beautiful Cassandra, who like her mother Hecuba, and the other Trojans Calchas and Laocoon had the gift of prophecy. But for Cassandra the gift was a curse, for she was doomed never to be believed.

When Cassandra was visiting Apollo's sanctuary one day, the god himself was struck by her beauty. As a mark of favour, he promised her the gift of prophecy. But when in return he sought to have his way with her, the young princess rebuffed his advances.

Apollo sought revenge. He could not take back his gift, for no divine edict could be undone; so instead he added a cruel rider to his bequest – that no one should ever believe her predictions.

From that time on, Cassandra could see only too clearly the tragedies that lay in store for her people. But whenever she sought to help them – by warning that Paris would bring calamity on Troy, for example, or that the Wooden Horse was a Greek ruse – she was greeted only with incredulity. Her name lives on to this day as a generic title for all those unfortunate enough to be able to foresee imminent disaster without being able to avert it.

When the Trojans got up next morning, they saw an astonishing sight from the ramparts of the city: only debris where the Greek camp had been, and in its place the gigantic wooden horse towering above the plain. Scouts sent out to examine this strange beast reported that it bore an inscription offering thanks from the Greeks to Athene in return for the promise of a safe journey home. Soon people were flocking out of the city to inspect the wonder. Most were suspicious of the horse, seeing a trap in it; and none more so than Laocoon, a priest of Apollo, who argued vehemently that this unwanted gift boded ill for Troy and must be destroyed at once.

But Odysseus had one more trick up his sleeve. He had left behind one of his followers, Sinon, dressed in rags and caked in mud. This man now made his appearance and was dragged before King Priam. Sinon had a story to tell. He pretended that he had learned the truth about Palamedes's death, and that Odysseus had sought to have him killed to stop him from spreading it. He had managed to escape from his would-be assassins, but the Greek ships had meanwhile set sail without him. If he made his own way home, only death would await him there. So he begged to be allowed to remain in Troy, and promised as an earnest of his good intentions to reveal the Greeks' final secret: that the wooden horse they had left behind was under the protection of Athene, and any city that received it within its walls could never be taken. That, he claimed, was why the Greeks had made it so large – to ensure that the Trojans could not pull it through any of their gates.

While the Trojans were weighing Sinon's words, an unforeseen event occurred that swung the balance of opinion in his favour. A pair of sea serpents, sent by Poseidon, slithered up from the shore and seized the two sons of the arch-sceptic Laocoon. The priest tried to rescue them, but all three were devoured. The onlookers at once deduced that these deaths were an omen. The gods had struck Laocoon down for his insolence towards Athene; and without more ado King Priam gave instructions for a section of the walls of Troy to be dismantled so the giant horse could enter the city.

It was a fatal error. That night, under cover of darkness, the Greek fleet left its hiding place behind Tenedos and sailed back to the Trojan shore. At the same time the warriors inside the horse slipped the catch and fanned out through

A warrior flings Hector's son Astyanax to his death while King Priam lies dying on the ground and Aphrodite protects Helen from the wrath of Menelaus in this depiction of the sack of Troy on a vase made in the 3rd century BC.

the streets of the sleeping city. Hurrying to its entrances, they slit the throats of the sentinels standing guard there and flung open the gates. By the time the Trojans realized what was happening, the streets were full of armed men. Soon the first fires were started.

What followed was butchery. Driven on by stories of the fabled wealth of Troy, the Greek soldiers embarked upon an orgy of rape and destruction. On soldiers and civilians alike, they took out all the frustrations built up in the course of nine years of war. Caught unawares, the Trojans were unable to put up any resistance. Before long the corpses of men, women and children littered the cobbles, and the gutters ran with blood.

Few of the Trojan leaders survived that terrible night. King Priam saw his son Polites cut down by Neoptolemus in the courtyard of his palace, and was then himself slain. Deiphobus, Helen's new husband, fell to the sword of his rival Menelaus. Hector's infant son Astyanax was captured alive, but the Greeks decided it would be too dangerous to let him remain so, and he was hurled to his death from the city walls. Among those who did escape were Antenor, protected by Odysseus in return for his honourable behaviour at the start of the siege, and Aeneas, whose subsequent adventures were themselves to become the stuff of legend (see pages 122–127).

Meanwhile the women of the court were assigned as slaves to the Greek victors. Hector's widow Andromache fell to Neoptolemus, while Queen Hecuba was given to Odysseus. The unhappy Cassandra was raped by the younger Ajax before Agamemnon's men seized her and took her to the king; but her violator did not go unpunished for the deed, for he was shipwrecked on the way home from Troy, and when he scrambled onto rocks to seek safety, Poseidon split them with his trident so that he drowned.

The fate of Cassandra's sister Polyxena was equally unhappy. She had taken Achilles's fancy many months before when he saw her on the walls of the city, and now the prophet Calchas declared that she must be sacrificed in tribute to

Despite her adultery, Helen's undiminished beauty inspired Menelaus's forgiveness when he found her. They sailed back to Greece and lived happily for many years. Their meeting is shown on the back of this 4th-century BC Etruscan bronze mirror.

the warrior's shade if the fleet was to have favourable winds for the journey back across the Aegean. Despite the prayers of her grieving mother Hecuba, she was dispatched at his tomb as the Greek army looked on.

As for Helen, Menelaus had intended to slay her for her infidelity, and there were many in the Greek army who wished him to do so. But one sight of her beauty was enough to change his mind, and he led her away in safety to the ships.

So the Greeks made ready for the voyage home. They took substantial amounts of booty, for though Troy's treasury had been depleted by the war it was still richly endowed. Yet few found pleasure in their arduously acquired wealth, for they had been away too long and they travelled back to a world that had changed in their absence.

A CITY THAT HISTORY FORGOT

Rome and Athens excepted, no town was better known by name in the classical world than Troy. The Troy with which the ancients were familiar was the city whose destruction Homer chronicled. A town of the same name grew up again near the same site, yet it never regained its former prominence and eventually disappeared from history. By the mid-nineteenth century, some scholars even doubted if it had ever really existed.

The man who saved Troy from obscurity was a tough and determined German businessman called Heinrich Schliemann. After making a fortune trading in indigo and in military supplies during the Crimean War, he gave up business and devoted his life to the archaeology of prehistory – and in particular the search for Troy.

Classical literature provided clear directions. The *Iliad* located Troy on what was by Schliemann's day Turkish territory, close to the southern mouth of the Dardanelles strait linking the Aegean and Black Seas. More specifically, ancient authors placed it on the flood-plain of the River Scamander – now the Menderes – in the shadow of Mount Ida, a 1750-metre peak known to the Turks as Kaz Dagi.

A visit to the area soon convinced Schliemann that the most likely site lay at a spot called Hisarlik. An English archaeologist named Frederick Calvert had made some preliminary investigations of a large man-made mound there. Schliemann took up his work in 1871, and within two years had unearthed fortifications and a treasure of gold jewellery that convinced him that he had found the Homeric city.

Schliemann and his successors eventually identified nine different layers of occupation at the site. The first five, dating from roughly 3000BC to 1900BC, were all the work of people of one culture. The big change came with Troy VI, which was settled from about 1900BC to 1300BC. This city was built by newcomers who brought with them horses – previously unknown to the region – and a new style of pottery. They were probably related to other invaders who were establishing the Mycenaean culture in Greece at around the same time.

The new city prospered. No doubt Troy benefited from its strategic location on the axis of trade routes; and to judge from the large number of spinning wheels found among its remains, it also became a centre for textile production.

Heinrich Schliemann saw a picture of Troy in flames in a history book as a child, and the image remained with him throughout his life. Even while he was making his fortune, he dreamed of rediscovering the lost city.

This level was for long taken to be Homer's city, but subsequent investigation was to disprove the theory. Troy VI was in fact destroyed not by a hostile army but by an earthquake. A new city soon rose on the same site, seemingly built by survivors of the earlier disaster.

Troy VIIA, as this layer is known, seems to have sheltered an even larger population than its predecessor, but it was to be short-lived. Within a generation it too had been razed. This time the city was burned, and the presence of human bones in the streets suggests it was put violently to the torch. This evidence, in conjunction with a date of around 1250BC – consistent with that given for the sack of Troy in classical sources – makes Troy VIIA the most likely contender to have been King Priam's city.

The so-called "Treasure of Priam", unearthed by Schliemann in 1873, comprised 250 gold objects which he later smuggled to Greece. Subsequent investigation has shown that many of the objects long predated the Trojan king.

Below: This 13cm-high clay urn was one of a number of vaguely human-featured vessels that Schliemann found in the early stages of his excavation of the city. Seeking evidence to link the finds with the Homeric city, he theorized that such objects may have represented "the Ilian Minerva crowned with an owl's head and surmounted by a kind of helmet". Today they are dated to 2600–1800BC, many centuries before Priam's day.

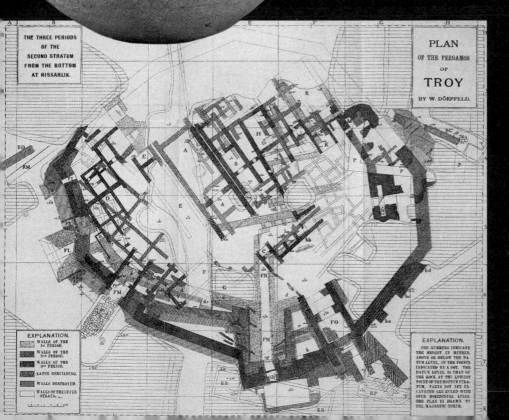

THE THREE PERIODS OF THE SECOND STRATUM FROM THE BOTTOM AT HISSARLIK.

PLAN OF THE PERGAMOS OF TROY BY W. DÖRPFELD.

EXPLANATION.
WALLS OF THE 1st PERIOD.
WALLS OF THE 2nd PERIOD.
WALLS OF THE 3rd PERIOD.
LATER REBUILDING.
WALLS DESTROYED.
WALLS OF THE UPPER STRATA.

EXPLANATION.
THE NUMBERS INDICATE THE HEIGHT IN METRES ABOVE OR BELOW THE DATUM LEVEL, OF THE POINTS INDICATED BY A DOT. THE DATUM LEVEL IS THAT OF THE ROCK AT THE LOWEST POINT OF THE BOTTOM STRATUM. PARTS NOT YET EXCAVATED ARE FILLED WITH OPEN HORIZONTAL LINES. THE PLAN IS DRAWN TO THE MAGNETIC NORTH.

Above: The components of this necklace, as well as the rings above it, were among the gold objects Schliemann dubbed "Priam's Treasure". Restored and restrung, they were presented to the world in a photograph, with the archaeologist's Greek wife Sophie as the model (inset). The treasure was displayed in Berlin until the end of World War II, when it went missing. Finally in 1994, Moscow's Pushkin Museum announced that it had the objects in its collections.

Left: A plan of Troy dating from 1891 shows the three levels of occupation identified to that day. At first Schliemann took the lowest stratum for the Homeric city. In fact current thinking dates Troy I back to about 2500BC, more than a millennium before the Trojan War.

Right: This clay mixing-bowl adorned with horns, dating from 1300–1100BC, was one of hundreds of vessels excavated by Schliemann. He sketched each one carefully in his journal, annotating the finds in several languages.

THE HEROES COME HOME

Classical myths that are centred on a heroic expedition or quest usually feature a return journey after the original goal has been achieved. Jason, Theseus and Perseus all returned home at the end of their travels, and in the same way the victors of the Trojan War – once Troy's resistance had finally been overcome and Helen had been won back – prepared for their voyages of return. In themselves, some of these journeys were to prove epic adventures. Destined to die in foreign lands, many of the Greek warriors were never to see their wives or homes again.

The longest and most elaborate return legend is that of Odysseus, retold in the *Odyssey*. Despite being persecuted by the sea god Poseidon, Odysseus survives a host of adventures. The drama of the action is increased by the tension between his roles on the one hand as an adventurer and on the other as a man with responsibilities – to his travelling comrades and to his waiting wife at home. The gods send him far out of his way, but always it is always clear that his true destiny lies in coming home. The *Odyssey* is the culmination of an ancient oral tradition in which bards sang long poems about the deeds of heroes to kings and their guests at great banquets. It is not known who the supposed author, Homer, was or whether a single author ever existed. The text of

the *Odyssey* seems to have come together in the eighth or seventh century BC and was written down around 650BC. Many of Odysseus's adventures were reworked from the tales of Jason and the Argonauts (see pages 36–45). Like Jason, Odysseus visits the witch Circe, sails past the enticing Sirens and survives the combined threats of Scylla and Charybdis.

Five hundred years later, the Roman poet Virgil used Odysseus's adventures as the model for those of his hero Aeneas, a Trojan warrior who travels to Italy and founds the Roman race. Writing at a time when Augustus Caesar had declared himself the first Emperor, Virgil was keenly aware of Rome's need to establish its pedigree as a great power by linking itself to the ancient civilization of the Greeks. Virgil described Aeneas's adventures in his great epic poem, the *Aeneid*. It is a work of literature in the modern sense, the product of a single mind. But the poet owed a debt to the scores of bards who, over hundreds of years, had polished, embellished and perfected the return myths of the heroes of the Trojan War.

Above: **A woman celebrates the harvest in this Mycenaean fresco. Just such a party must have been thrown on the heroes' return.**

Opposite: **A detail from a Roman mosaic shows Odysseus and his men sailing safely past the island of the Sirens who, with sweet songs, tried to lure passers-by to their deaths. Odysseus is tied to the mast; his sailors' ears are blocked.**

109

Many Ways from Troy to Greece

The Greek heroes preparing to sail from Troy after achieving their great task were looking forward to returning home after their long exile. Some launched their ships and others made the journey over land, but the fate of all remained in the hands of the fickle gods.

As the Greeks massed on the beach before Troy, a quarrel sprang up between Menelaus – who wanted to set sail for home straight away – and his brother Agamemnon, who was determined to stay awhile in order to make sacrifices to Athene. The goddess was furious at the Greek violation of her sanctuary at Troy during the battle.

Aware of Athene's anger, some Greeks set out on foot to avoid disaster at sea. Diomedes and Nestor agreed to leave with Menelaus. They set sail together, and the first two arrived home quickly – but Athene punished Menelaus by sending a storm which destroyed most of his fleet (see box opposite). When Agamemnon finally set sail he took the Trojan princess, Cassandra, with him.

Agamemnon's wife Clytemnestra heard that he was returning with Cassandra and she plotted with her lover Aegisthus to kill him. There are different versions of how Agamemnon met his death. In the *Odyssey*, Aegisthus invited the returning king to a great feast. After they had eaten, Aegisthus and his men slaughtered Agamemnon and his followers. None were left alive.

In the version told by the Greek playwright Aeschylus in the fifth century BC, Clytemnestra welcomed Agamemnon and led him to the bathhouse, where he washed the grime from his weary body. As the king came out of the bath she threw a net over him. Aegisthus stepped forward and killed him with a double-edged sword; Clytemnestra then hacked off Agamemnon's head and murdered Cassandra with the same bloody weapon.

When the 19th-century German archaeologist Heinrich Schliemann found this gold funeral mask at the site of Mycenae, he exclaimed: "I have gazed upon the face of Agamemnon." In fact the mask predates the Trojan Wars by at least 300 years.

Menelaus Waits for Fair Winds

Menelaus set sail from Troy for his kingdom of Sparta with his wife Helen, whose elopement with a Trojan lover had precipitated the long and bloody war. His stubborn refusal to make sacrifices to the goddess Athene before leaving plunged him, Helen and their companions into trouble at once.

Leaving Troy with Diomedes and Nestor, Menelaus was separated from them in a great storm and his fleet was devastated. The five ships that survived were blown to Egypt, where they were becalmed for eight years.

On the island of Pharos, Menelaus met the sea-nymph Eidoethea. She told him that he must capture her father Proteus, the shepherd of fish and other sea animals, who knew all things, past, present and future. He would tell Menelaus how to raise a wind to sail home.

Menelaus and three followers disguised themselves as seals on a beach and when Proteus came out of the waves and lay down to sleep they leaped upon him. The god tried to escape by changing form, becoming a lion, a snake and even a stream, but Menelaus would not let go. Finally Proteus told Menelaus of Agamemnon's murder (see main text) and that Odysseus was being held against his will by the sea nymph Calypso (see page 117). He instructed Menelaus to return to Egypt and make a sacrifice to the gods. When he did this, a wind came up that carried him home.

Menelaus and Helen came to Mycenae, where they found that in an act of revenge Agamemnon's son Orestes had killed his father's murderers, Clytemnestra and Aegisthus, and was now facing trial and possible death. Orestes appealed for help but Menelaus refused. Orestes and his sister Electra then seized Helen and tried to kill her, but she was rescued by Aphrodite. Helen and Menelaus travelled on to Sparta, where they settled. When Telemachus came there seeking news of his father Odysseus (see page 119), he found them living happily together. On his death Menelaus was made immortal by the gods and was allowed to go to the Elysian Fields, the realm of the blessed, with Helen.

Odysseus, the Wandering Hero

The warrior Odysseus was famed above all for his quick wits. It had been his ingenious plan that finally brought the ten-year siege of the city to an end (see page 100). The battle done, he set out from Troy for Ithaca and his beloved wife, Penelope, but many perils lay ahead. He needed all his intelligence and resourcefulness to survive them.

Odysseus was impatient to be home in Ithaca, but soon after he set sail from Troy storms blew his fleet off course and he came to land in Thrace. With his followers he attacked and burned the city of the Cicones, putting the men who defended it to the sword, but he spared Maro, a priest of Apollo, who gave the hero several skins of sweet wine. As Odysseus and his followers rested on the beach, Ciconians from further inland launched a savage reprisal raid, killing many Greeks and forcing the others to flee by sea.

Winds drove the fleet to the land of the Lotus-Eaters, in Libya. When three sailors went ashore to look for a supply of fresh water, the locals gave them pieces of their delicate fruit. Its heady taste made the travellers forget about their home and yearn to stay exactly where they were for ever. But eventually Odysseus and some followers went looking for the missing men. They, too, were tempted to stay and taste the fruit, but they managed to restrain themselves. Grabbing their shipmates, they dragged them back to the vessel.

They next came to the land of the Cyclopes, a breed of terrifying giants each with a single, vast eye in the centre of his forehead. Odysseus and

Poseidon, god of the sea – and enemy of Odysseus – features in this 2nd-century mosaic from Tunisia.

some of his men went ashore and came upon an inviting cave where they found young goats in a corner and cheeses hung from the walls. They lit a fire, killed some of the goats and settled down to feast, little realizing that the animals belonged to a Cyclops named Polyphemus – son of the sea god Poseidon. A shepherd by trade, Polyphemus loved the taste of human flesh.

Polyphemus returned with his flock and rolled a great stone across the entrance. Seeing his uninvited guests, he demanded brusquely who they were. Odysseus asked for hospitality, reminding the giant that it was a matter of honour before the gods to greet strangers kindly, but Polyphemus only grunted, grabbed two of the sailors and smashed their heads on their floor before devouring them with a crunching of bones.

A Deed Done by Nobody

The following morning the Cyclops breakfasted on two more men before driving off his herd and closing the cave again with the stone. Odysseus, ever cunning, devised a plan. While Polyphemus was away the hero found a long stake, sharpened it and hid it beneath some animal dung in the corner of the cave. In the evening the Cyclops returned and devoured two more unlucky sailors, but then Odysseus stepped forward, offering the monster a bowl of the wine that Maro had given the Greeks in Cicones. Polyphemus poured it down his great throat and growled with pleasure. Three times he asked the stranger to refill the bowl – then, becoming drunk, asked his name. The hero replied that it was "Nobody". Polyphemus promised that he would eat "Nobody" last, then he crashed to the floor in a drunken stupor and vomited a stream of wine and human flesh.

Odysseus and his men seized their chance. They heated the stake in the fire and rammed it into the monster's single eye, twisting it with all their strength. Polyphemus's eyeball boiled and hissed, and he gave a frightful shriek. A band of Cyclopes gathered at the entrance of the cave, asking what was the matter. Polyphemus roared "Nobody is hurting me", so they went away. When the blinded Cyclops rolled back the stone to let his flock out, Odysseus and his men escaped by tying themselves under the bellies of the sheep, hiding in their shaggy wool. The monster ran his hands over the animals' backs, but he did not notice the Greeks clinging on underneath.

They reached the safety of the ships, and Odysseus triumphantly shouted out his true name. Then the Cyclops hurled a vast rock at the hero's ship, creating a wave that almost washed it ashore

once more, and he prayed to his father Poseidon to bring grief and trouble to Odysseus.

The fleet sailed on and visited Aeolus, the keeper of the winds. He gave Odysseus a bag of winds, and sent up a westerly breeze that blew the Greeks all the way home. The ships were so close to Ithaca that smoke could be seen from the palace chimneys when Odysseus, exhausted, fell asleep. In that fatal moment some of the Greek sailors, thinking that the bag contained gold, untied it. A great tempest was unleashed that blew them far out to sea again.

Then they were driven to the land of the Laestrygonian giants. Most of the ships anchored in

Scholars disagree about exactly where Odysseus had his adventures and about which locations are entirely mythical. This map shows one possible reconstruction of his route and of his son Telemachus's journey around the Peloponnese.

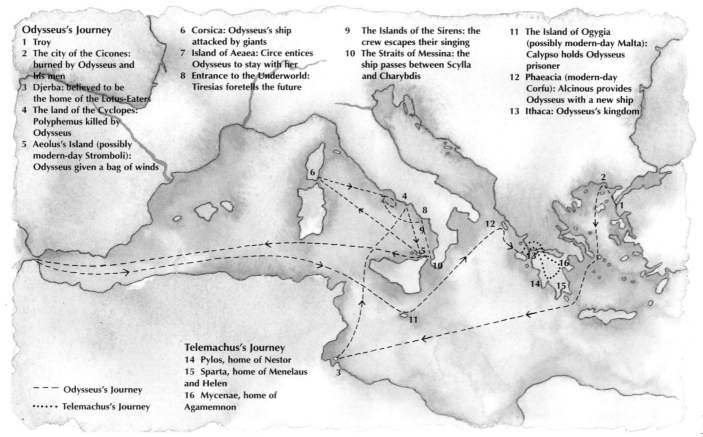

Odysseus's Journey
1 Troy
2 The city of the Cicones: burned by Odysseus and his men
3 Djerba: believed to be the home of the Lotus-Eaters
4 The land of the Cyclops: Polyphemus killed by Odysseus
5 Aeolus's Island (possibly modern-day Stromboli): Odysseus given a bag of winds
6 Corsica: Odysseus's ship attacked by giants
7 Island of Aeaea: Circe entices Odysseus to stay with her
8 Entrance to the Underworld: Tiresias foretells the future
9 The Islands of the Sirens: the crew escapes their singing
10 The Straits of Messina: the ship passes between Scylla and Charybdis
11 The Island of Ogygia (possibly modern-day Malta): Calypso holds Odysseus prisoner
12 Phaeacia (modern-day Corfu): Alcinous provides Odysseus with a new ship
13 Ithaca: Odysseus's kingdom

Telemachus's Journey
14 Pylos, home of Nestor
15 Sparta, home of Menelaus and Helen
16 Mycenae, home of Agamemnon

- - - Odysseus's Journey
· · · · · Telemachus's Journey

a harbour, but Odysseus stayed further out. Three of the sailors went ashore, where they were immediately attacked. Then the giants pelted the ships in the harbour with boulders – and harpooned the men for their supper.

Odysseus's ship was the only one to escape this massacre. He sailed on to Aeaea, where some of the sailors went inland, and found the witch Circe in her palace. She invited them in to eat, and they all agreed except one, Eurylochus, who was afraid it might be a trap. He watched his friends tuck into a drugged meal; Circe then used a magic wand to transform the sailors into pigs. Eurylochus raced back to the ship and told Odysseus, who grabbed his sword and set out to seek revenge. Protected by an enchanted flower given to him by Hermes, the gods' messenger, Odysseus was immune to Circe's spells. He made her promise not to use any spells against him and to return the sailors to human form. But then she enticed him to stay; he became her lover, and the sailors stayed on the island for a whole year.

Odysseus Raises the Dead

Finally, Ithaca beckoned, and Circe – accepting that Odysseus was determined to leave – told him to seek out the blind prophet Tiresias, who would tell him how to return home. She instructed him to sail to the edge of the world, dig a trench and fill it with offerings. Then he should sacrifice a ram and a black ewe in honour of Hades and Persephone, the king and queen of the Underworld, to summon the prophet.

Odysseus sailed to the land of perpetual darkness and carried out Circe's instructions. As Odysseus poured blood into the trench, the souls of the dead – girls, young men, old men and

warriors with their wounds still gaping – came swarming up from underground with a gibbering sound. Terrified, Odysseus fended them off with his sword until Tiresias came forward.

A Stern Prophecy, a Grim Encounter

Tiresias foretold that the sailors would land on the island of Thrinacia, where Helios the sun god kept cattle, which must on no account be eaten. He said that Odysseus would reach Ithaca but would find

The beautiful sorceress Circe, complete with wand and potion, strides across a Greek ochre-figure vase from the 5th century BC. She had the power to change men into wolves, lions, pigs and other animals.

A Race of Beastly Shepherds

The Cyclopes, fearsome one-eyed giants, occur in the Odyssey and in early Greek myths of the creation of the world.

In the *Theogeny*, an account of the origins of the gods written by the Greek poet Hesiod in the eighth century BC, the original Cyclopes were three sons of Uranos (Heaven) and Gaia (Earth). Uranos threw them down into the abyss of Tartarus, and in revenge Gaia persuaded her other sons, the Titans, to castrate him.

A widespread tradition placed the Cyclopes in Sicily, where Polyphemus was said to have fallen in love with the nymph Galatea. Just as he was stupid and cruel in his dealings with Odysseus (see pages 112–113), so he was uncouth and boorish with Galatea – and she did not return his love. In one version, Polyphemus crushed his rival Acis to death with a stone. This was the version followed in the opera *Acis and Galatea* by the eighteenth-century composer Georg Friedrich Handel.

Cyclopes were also said to have built the walls of Mycenae and Tiryns, whose stone blocks were thought too large to have been set there by human hands. The term "Cyclopean" is still used to describe massive stone structures.

A prosperous Roman of the 4th century AD installed in his villa this mosaic of Polyphemus greedily accepting a bowl of Thracian wine from Odysseus. Perhaps he intended it as a wry caution against drinking too much.

great trouble there – and that his travels would not be over. He would have to set out once more, inland, carrying an oar on his shoulders until he met men who were so unfamiliar with the sea that they did not recognize it as an oar. But he would have a peaceful death in old age. In some versions of the myth Tiresias also prophesied that Odysseus's death would come from the sea.

Among the spirits that swarmed around him, Odysseus was shocked to see the pale ghost of his mother, Anticlea, because he did not know that she was dead. As soon as she drank the dark blood from the trench she recognized her son's features, and told him that she had died of grief at his long absence from Ithaca. Odysseus tried three times to embrace her but his arms passed through her shadowy body. He also spoke with many former comrades from the wars at Troy, including the great warrior Achilles, who mournfully said that he would far rather be a peasant working the land beneath the sun than live among the dead, even with great power. He met Agamemnon, who – recalling his own violent and terrible homecoming (see page 110) – warned Odysseus to return to

Ithaca in disguise. But finally the clamour of the dead swarming around them became so great that the sailors fled back to the ship.

They returned to Aeaea, where Circe gave them a warm welcome and advised Odysseus how to pass safely through the perils that still lay ahead. Once the Greeks set sail from her island their first trial was to pass the Sirens, whose unbearably lovely singing lured men to their deaths. Following Circe's advice, Odysseus filled his sailors' ears with beeswax so that they could not hear the songs; he planned to keep his own ears open, and ordered the men to tie him as tightly as they could to the mast – warning them that on no account should they release him. When they sailed past the Sirens, Odysseus was desperate to be free and gestured frantically to the men to untie him – but they only pulled the knots tighter. The ship sailed on and the Sirens, maddened by their failure, hurled themselves into the water where they drowned.

Next the sailors had to pass between Scylla and Charybdis. Scylla was a monster with six heads on long necks, who squatted on a cliff and snatched sailors as they passed. Charybdis sucked in a vast amount of water three times each day, creating a whirlpool capable of swallowing ships that sailed too close. In his concern to avoid Charybdis, Odysseus sailed a little too near to Scylla and the monster leant down and snatched six of his finest sailors – one in each mouth. The men howled and begged to be rescued but Odysseus, powerless to help them, sailed on.

The male nude was an important theme in Roman art. The story of Odysseus offered sculptors – like the creator of this powerful figure from the 1st century AD – plenty of opportunities to demonstrate their skill.

The sailors then came to the island of Thrinacia, home of Helios, the sun god. Odysseus reminded his men that Tiresias had warned of terrible danger if they ate the god's cattle, and said that they should sail on, but the crew insisted on putting in. During the night, the wind changed and the sailors were trapped there for a whole month. Food ran low and the men were starving, and while Odysseus was asleep Eurylochus and the others slaughtered and roasted some of the beasts. When Odysseus awoke he was furious with his men, but they feasted for six days and then, in calm weather, set sail once more.

Helios was livid and complained to Zeus, who promised to destroy the sailors. He attacked the ship with a terrible storm and all on board were drowned – except Odysseus, who made a raft from the floating timbers. After escaping the whirlpool of Charybdis again, the hero drifted for nine days, coming to land finally on the island of Ogygia, home to the beautiful sea nymph Calypso ("The Concealer"). She fell in love with the handsome castaway and, after giving him food and wine, seduced him. Calypso held Odysseus prisoner on the island for seven years, but he soon grew tired of her and would sit staring forlornly out to sea, longing for home.

Athene Secures the Hero's Freedom

On Mount Olympus the gods noticed Odysseus's plight. All felt sorry for the hero except Poseidon, who hated him for blinding his son Polyphemus. When Poseidon went to faraway Ethiopia to receive a sacrifice, Athene seized the opportunity presented by his absence. She persuaded Zeus to help Odysseus. The father of the gods dispatched his messenger, Hermes, to Ogygia. Hermes gave Calypso the message she had long been dreading: Odysseus had suffered enough and Zeus was ordering her to let him go. Unwillingly, she helped Odysseus build a ship and gave him provisions for the journey. Odysseus had grown fond of her, but he had never forgotten his goal of returning home to his wife. He was glad to set sail again.

Eighteen days later, as Odysseus sailed past the land of Phaeacia (modern Corfu), Poseidon returned from his prolonged revels in Ethiopia. Enraged at the sight of his enemy in full sail, he seized his trident, stirring up an immense storm which smashed Odysseus's ship and would have killed him if a sea nymph had not taken pity and helped him to shore. Poseidon vowed to punish him again another day. Naked and scratched from being dragged over jagged rocks, Odysseus finally clambered ashore by a stream. There, exhausted, he fell asleep under some bushes.

Rescued by a Princess

He woke to the sound of shrieking girls. Covering himself with a branch, he crept out from under the bushes to find a young princess playing ball with her maidservants. The other girls fled at the sight of the grimy, naked stranger, but Athene made the princess stand firm while Odysseus threw himself at her knees, asking for pity. She gave him food and fresh clothes, and while he washed and dressed himself, she whispered to her maids that such a handsome man would make a perfect husband. Then, raising her voice, she told Odysseus that she was Nausicaa – daughter of Phaeacia's king, Alcinous – and invited him to the palace. She said he could walk with her until they were close to the city, but then, to avoid malicious gossip, she should go on ahead while he approached the palace as a stranger. When he arrived there, she said, he should go straight in to her mother and clasp her knees in supplication.

Odysseus did as Nausicaa told him, impressing the queen and King Alcinous with his noble bearing and speech. Following local custom, the king offered Odysseus a ship in which to sail home. The next day, while sailors were preparing the vessel, Alcinous entertained Odysseus at a magnificent feast. There was a display of sports and dancing, and then the blind bard Demodocus stepped forward to entertain the diners with songs of the Trojan War. When the bard recounted Odysseus's own adventures, the hero wept.

117

Still not suspecting his true identity, Alcinous asked Odysseus who he was. In a long and moving speech, Odysseus told the guests of his adventures since he had left Troy. Although the whole world marvelled at his exploits, he said, he was in reality a wretched man whose only desire was to return to his island home of Ithaca. When Odysseus finished his tale, there was silence throughout the shadowy hall. Finally Alcinous spoke up, promising to send the hero home.

Odysseus Sleeps All the Way Home

The next morning, laden with gifts, Odysseus set sail from Phaeacia. He was so exhausted that he fell asleep on the voyage, and when the ship reached Ithaca the Phaeacian sailors laid him down on the beach, still slumbering.

When he awoke the ship was gone, and Athene appeared to tell him that he was in Ithaca. Warning him to keep his true identity secret, she

A beach scene at Corfu, where Odysseus was washed ashore. He was welcomed by King Alcinous and his family, who feasted him and eventually sent him home to Ithaca in a new ship.

disguised him as a ragged beggar and sent him to stay with his loyal servant Eumaeus. Odysseus pretended to be a refugee from Crete when he arrived at Eumaeus's hut, and he received a warm welcome. Eumaeus told the stranger that more than a hundred princes, presuming that Odysseus was dead, had invaded the king's palace and remained there, eating his food, drinking his wine and pestering his wife Penelope to marry one of them. At this moment Odysseus's son Telemachus, back from Sparta (see box opposite), appeared in the doorway of the hut. Odysseus was moved to see Eumaeus embrace Telemachus like a son.

Eumaeus hurried away to tell Penelope of Telemachus's return, leaving the father and son alone. Then Athene removed Odysseus's disguise,

Telemachus Sets Forth

Odysseus's son Telemachus was a baby when his father left for the Trojan War. He grew up into a fine young man, but he could not control the suitors who invaded his father's palace and pestered his mother Penelope to marry one of them.

The goddess Athene arrived at the palace of Ithaca disguised as a foreign king and told Telemachus to send the suitors home. Then he must sail to Pylos and Sparta in search of news of his father. After she finished speaking, Athene vanished through the roof – and Telemachus, realizing who she was, was greatly heartened.
He summoned the suitors and berated them about their conduct, begging them to go home. The suitors' leader, Antinous, retorted that they would not leave until Penelope agreed to marry one of them.

Telemachus decided to set off secretly to Pylos. Athene went round the city to find a ship and recruit the crew. Then, assuming the form of Odysseus's old friend Mentor, she led Telemachus to the ship and joined him on board.

Telemachus and Athene, in Mentor's disguise, soon reached Pylos, where they were received by King Nestor. He regaled them with tales of Odysseus's bravery, but knew nothing about his fate. Nestor gave Telemachus a chariot and his best horses, with his son as companion. Athene turned back, while the young men drove on to Sparta.

There Menelaus entertained his guests to a feast. When Helen entered the room she knew at once that Telemachus must be Odysseus's son. Telemachus asked Menelaus if he knew what had become of his father. Menelaus said that on his return from Troy he had become stuck in Egypt (see page 111) where Proteus, the Old Man of the Sea, told him that he had seen a tearful Odysseus trapped on an island by the nymph Calypso.

The suitors back on Ithaca sent another ship to ambush Telemachus on his return journey and kill him. But Athene was able to warn the prince and he came home by a different route to find his father, disguised as a beggar, already home.

and told him to reveal himself to his son. At first Telemachus thought that Odysseus was some god and would not believe him, but then he was overcome by tears and the reunited pair embraced tenderly. They made plans to avenge themselves on the suitors, and Telemachus returned immediately to the palace.

Odysseus again disguised himself as a beggar so that when Eumaeus returned he still did not recognize his master. But Eumaeus agreed to take Odysseus to the palace to beg, which was a common practice at the time. This gave Odysseus the chance to find out what kind of men he was up against. He soon discovered that they were low and cowardly. The suitors' ringleader, Antinous, grossly insulted the newcomer, striking him on the back with a stool.

Later that afternoon Penelope made an announcement. To the delight of her suitors, she said that she had at last accepted that her husband Odysseus must be dead, and would marry one of them. After a long evening of feasting and boasting, the suitors finally retired to bed. Odysseus and Telemachus now began to put their plan into action, taking down all the weapons and armour which hung around the walls of the hall.

Odysseus Keeps up the Deception

Penelope came downstairs and sat by the fire to question the visitor for news of her husband, confessing that she had used a device to avoid marrying the suitors. She said that she would only remarry when she had finished weaving a shroud for Odysseus's father, Laertes. She had made this task last for three years, unpicking at night what she sewed by day. The beggar told her that he had fought at Troy, and had seen Odysseus. Tears flowed down her cheeks, but Odysseus managed

The loyal Eumaeus, seen in a 5th-century BC terracotta image, had royal blood – he was a prince who was sold into slavery.

with an effort to hold his own emotions in check. Now Odysseus's old nurse Eurycleia brought a bowl to bathe the guest. He turned away from the light to avoid recognition, but she noticed a familiar scar above his knee. With a gasp she upset the bowl and spilled the water. She was about to call out to Penelope when Odysseus clamped his hand over her mouth and made her swear to keep his identity secret.

The next day, Penelope announced that she had devised a test to select her new husband. She would marry whichever man could string Odysseus's great bow and shoot an arrow straight through a row of twelve axes. A vast feast was laid out, the bow was carried in and the contest began. One after another, the suitors tried but could not even bend the bow, let alone string it and shoot an arrow. Odysseus, still in disguise, asked if he might try the bow.

While the suitors laughed and abused him, Telemachus sent his mother and the other women to their quarters, with instructions to lock their doors and ignore any sounds from the hall. While loyal servants took up stations barring the exit doors, Odysseus weighed the massive bow in his hands, turning it this way and that.

He strung the bow effortlessly. Unhurriedly, Odysseus fitted an arrow to the string and fired it. The arrow passed right through the twelve axes. As Telemachus appeared by his side in full armour with sword and spear, Odysseus fired a second arrow. It pierced Antinous in the throat, just as he was lifting up a golden cup, and his life-blood gushed from his nostrils as he kicked over his table and fell choking to the floor.

There was uproar in the hall. Thinking that Odysseus had killed Antinous by accident, the suitors leapt to their feet. Their blood ran cold as they saw that the weapons on the walls had disappeared. Odysseus spoke out in a ringing voice, revealing his true identity. The desperate suitors pleaded with him, offering him compensation for all the food and wine they had consumed, but Odysseus was implacable. He fired again and again, his sure shot felling them one by one.

Telemachus, Eumaeus and another loyal servant were at Odysseus's side as he slowly drove the surviving suitors down the hall, massacring them till they lay in heaps like fish on a beach. Then they rounded up the servants who had been disloyal and executed them. The nurse Eurycleia ran upstairs to tell Penelope that her husband was back. But Penelope was still too shocked to believe her. She came downstairs, wondering whether to remain aloof or to rush forward and kiss the man whose identity she still doubted. She sat down quietly on the far side of the hall, gazing at him as he, too, sat in wary silence.

Odysseus spoke first, saying that if his wife would not talk to him at least she could make up a bed for him to sleep alone. But now the shrewd Penelope put him to the test. She called to her servants to move out the great bed that Odysseus had built himself. Odysseus leapt to his feet, reminding her that the bed could not possibly be moved because he had constructed it around a living olive tree – a secret that was known only to the two of them.

Realizing that her husband had returned, she flung her arms around him, saying she had been afraid of being deceived. They went joyously to bed, and after making love they recounted the difficulties they had endured during their long years apart.

Knowing that he had to win the forgiveness of Poseidon, the sea god, Odysseus travelled inland, as instructed by Tiresias. He came to a place far from the sea, where he sacrificed a boar, a bull and a ram to the god. His task accomplished, he returned to his palace and lived happily with Penelope into great old age.

Penelope fails to recognize her husband, disguised as a beggar. This 5th-century BC terracotta relief was found on Melos, an island renowned for its artworks.

Aeneas, Founder of the Roman Race

The Trojan prince Aeneas was a son of Venus, the Roman goddess of love – known to the Greeks as Aphrodite. Before he was born the goddess prophesied that her son would come to rule over the Trojans and would found a great and undying dynasty. He was a leading Trojan warrior in the war against the Greeks, but when Troy was sacked he fled the city's smoking ruins and set out across the seas to fulfil his destiny.

On the night Troy fell, the Greek soldiers rampaged through the city like marauding wolves, spreading panic and death. Aeneas fought desperately, but when he saw the Trojan king Priam killed, he realized that the city was lost. Taking his young son Ascanius by the hand he lifted his father Anchises onto his shoulder and carried him out of the blazing ruins. Aeneas's wife Creusa followed, but was lost in the turmoil and confusion. When, in desperation, Aeneas went back to look for her he saw a vision of Creusa in which she told him to give up the search and flee to safety.

After a stay on Mount Ida, near Troy – where they built ships and prepared for a sea voyage – the Trojans set out for Thrace. There Aeneas was met by the ghost of Priam's son Polydorus, who told him he had to leave. They carried on to Delos to consult the oracle of Apollo who told Aeneas that he must find the "ancient mother" of his people. Anchises said that the oracle must mean Crete – homeland of Teucer, an ancestor of Troy's founder.

When they reached Crete Aeneas had a dream revealing that the oracle actually referred to Italy, home of Dardanus, another of his ancestors. The next stop for the Trojan ships was Epirus on Greece's western coast, where a Trojan prophet, Helenus, advised Aeneas to travel on to

Sicily. They sailed on past Scylla and Charybdis, the twin monsters that threatened the wandering hero Odysseus on his travels (see page 116), but when they reached Sicily, Anchises died, worn out by the long and arduous voyage. Stricken with grief, Aeneas buried his father at Drepanum, close to Eryx where a shrine already stood in honour of his immortal mother Venus.

Juno, the Roman version of Hera, hated Aeneas because he was a Trojan. Here she is depicted in marble by a follower of Praxiteles in the 4th century BC.

The Goddesses Interfere

The goddess Juno had learned that Aeneas was destined to found a race so great that it would one day destroy Carthage, a city on the shores of Tunisia, northern Africa, that she favoured above all others. When Aeneas's fleet set sail from Sicily, heading for mainland Italy, she ordered Aeolus, the keeper of the winds, to release hurricanes. Aeneas watched in despair as many of his ships were sunk in a huge storm.

The survivors were driven to Carthage, where Queen Dido welcomed them with a vast banquet. After the food Aeneas recounted his adventures, starting with the tale of the Trojan horse and the fall of Troy, and describing all his wanderings since then. Venus, wanting to help Aeneas, sent Cupid to make Dido fall in love with him. The love magic worked. As she listened spellbound to Aeneas's narrative, Dido's veins began to burn and later, ablaze with passion, she rushed frenziedly about the city like a deer pierced by an arrowhead.

Juno saw that this was a chance to divert Aeneas from his destiny in Italy. The next day, as Dido and Aeneas set out on a hunt, the goddess sent a rainstorm. The hunt retinue scattered in the torrential downpour and Dido and Aeneas found themselves alone in a cave, where they made love. But Jupiter sent his messenger Mercury to remind Aeneas of his great destiny and instruct him to leave Carthage at once.

Aeneas did not know how to break the news to Dido. When she heard that the fleet was being prepared she flew into a rage, calling Aeneas traitor and threatening to hound him wherever he went. Aeneas was torn by inner conflict, but the call of destiny stiffened his resolve.

The grief-stricken queen asked her sister Anna to build a huge pyre, saying that she needed to burn every object that reminded her of Aeneas – in particular a sword that he had left behind. Later that same night Mercury, the gods' messenger, told Aeneas in a dream that he must sail before daybreak. As Dido watched his ships slipping away in the dawn she cursed him to a hard journey and his descendants to a long history of future warfare with the city of Carthage. Then she climbed the pyre she had made of her lover's belongings and threw herself on Aeneas's sword. Her body was burned to ashes soon afterwards. Far out at sea, the Trojans looked back to Carthage and saw the thick column of smoke, without knowing its terrible meaning.

Aeneas Lands in Italy

When the Trojans came to Sicily once more, they stopped to stage funeral games in honour of Aeneas's late father Anchises. There Juno incited some of the Trojans to burn their ships and settle; they founded the city of Egesta. But the goddess could not prevent the remainder from pushing on to mainland Italy. They landed at Cumae, near Naples, where Aeneas sought out the Sibyl, an ancient prophetess. She warned him that a hard road lay ahead, with terrible wars in Italy. Aeneas begged to be allowed to visit the Underworld, in order to see his beloved father once more. The prophetess warned him that the descent to Hades was easy, but the return was hard. She agreed to escort him to the land of the dead and told him to find a branch of the sacred mistletoe which would be their pass.

They set out in pitch darkness through the insubstantial shadows of the Underworld. At length they came to the banks of the Styx, where they saw Charon the ferryman roughly pushing back the souls of the dead as they pressed forward, desperate to be taken across. Charon agreed to carry Aeneas and the Sibyl, although their living weight made his barge sit dangerously low in the murky water.

Disembarking on the other side they first passed the spirits of those who had died in childhood, then the ghosts of suicides. Next they came to the phantoms of those who had died for love. Dido was there and Aeneas tried to tell her that he loved her and had been forced to leave her against his will in order to follow his fate, but she only turned away. The Sibyl drew Aeneas on, past the fields of war heroes, where he spoke with many friends, and past the river of fire that surrounded those condemned to an eternity of punishment.

Anchises Shows Aeneas the Future

Finally they reached the green and pleasant abode of the blessed, where the light was radiant and the air fresh. Aeneas's father Anchises saw him coming and cried out with joy. With tears running down his cheeks, Aeneas tried to embrace his beloved father – but his arms passed right through his ghostly body. Anchises explained the mysteries of death, purification and reincarnation, showing him

Mercury had to remind Aeneas of his destiny. The gods' messenger, depicted in this Roman bronze, was called Hermes by the Greeks.

a line of souls preparing to be born. These were Aeneas's own descendants who would one day carry Rome to glory (see box, page 126). His father told him that they would arise from his future marriage to an Italian princess named Lavinia. Aeneas gazed in astonishment before his father took him and the Sibyl to the gate that led back to the upper world.

Aeneas rejoined his crew and they sailed on to Latium, at the mouth of the River Tiber. The king, Latinus, had recently dreamt that a stranger would marry his daughter Lavinia, and that their union would give rise to a great nation. But Latinus had already promised Lavinia to Turnus, king of the local Rutulian tribe. However, when he received a messenger from Aeneas, he remembered his dream and offered the princess to him instead. Juno, still looking for opportunities to cause trouble for the Trojans, decided to work through the spurned suitor Turnus. She stirred up a brawl between Latins and Trojans in which two Latins were killed. The local tribes, including Latinus and his people, united under Turnus to expel the Trojan interlopers.

The Latin armies massed on the banks of the Tiber, and the watching Aeneas felt a great surge of despair, for the Trojans were heavily outnumbered. But then the god of the river Tiber advised Aeneas in a dream to visit Evander, the king of nearby Arcadia, and to make an alliance with him. Evander agreed to lend his support, undertaking to bring the Etruscans into the alliance. As a token of trust he sent his beloved son Pallas back with Aeneas, putting the youth under his personal protection.

As if to seal the bargain, Aeneas's mother Venus appeared in a clap of thunder to present Aeneas with a magnificent shield made by the

124

divine craftsman Vulcan. This shield, she said, would make her son invincible in battle. Yet Juno was not to be thwarted. She warned Turnus that Aeneas was away, canvassing support. Turnus swooped down on the Trojan camp, and mounted a surprise attack. And so the battle began.

Aeneas returned with Arcadian and Etruscan reinforcements and the fighting continued. In a tragic moment, Turnus killed Evander's son Pallas – and exuberantly pulled the belt from Pallas's body and donned it himself as a trophy. Aeneas had no quarrel with Latinus, who had received him kindly and offered him his daughter, and suggested that, to save bloodshed, he and Turnus should meet in single combat. Turnus agreed, although Latinus's wife Amata tried to dissuade him. She was fond of Turnus and still wanted him to marry Lavinia.

Juno was still determined to do whatever she could to wreak havoc among the Trojans. She warned Turnus's sister, Juturna, that her brother would die in an encounter with Aeneas and

Rome's Debt to Troy

In Homer's account of the Trojan War, the **Iliad**, *Aeneas is not a major figure. When the Roman poet Virgil identified him as the founder of the Roman dynasty he was following a tradition dating from the third century BC, two hundred years before his own day.*

In the *Iliad* the Trojan warrior Aeneas fought many times against the Greek heroes, but was always saved by the gods for a higher purpose. The Greek mythical tradition describes him as surviving the slaughter when Troy fell. "The Fall of Troy" – a cyclic poem, now lost – claimed that Aeneas left the city before it was overrun and took his family to Mount Ida. By the sixth century BC, he was widely depicted on vases carrying his father out of the ruins. There were various versions of his wanderings, but all showed him moving towards Italy. But the interlude with Dido is probably not traditional. It may have been invented by Virgil to explain Rome's hostility to Carthage, home of the great general Hannibal who waged war on Rome in the third century BC.

This gladiator's helmet is decorated with scenes from the sack of Troy, a tale that would have been familiar to every educated citizen of Rome. Fighters in the Coliseum would have been proud to identify themselves with the Greeks.

Aeneas, Ancestor of Augustus

In 31BC, after thirty years of civil war, Augustus defeated Anthony and Cleopatra and became the supreme ruler of the Roman world, giving himself the new title of Emperor. One of Virgil's aims in the Aeneid was to glorify Augustus. The poet represents Aeneas as the Emperor's political precursor as well as his ancestor; both men brought peace to an age that was exhausted by civil war.

Gaius Julius Caesar Octavianus chose the name "Augustus" – meaning "Sacred" – to boost his status. The Romans declared him "Father of His Country" in 2BC. When he died he was transformed into a god.

Virgil may well have found some aspects of Augustus's totalitarian rule distasteful, but he accepted his official patronage and portrayed the Emperor's reign as the culmination of a thousand years of history and prophecy.

Aeneas, like Augustus, had a mission to make Rome glorious. When he met Anchises in the Underworld his father showed him the line of his descendants, among whom was Augustus Caesar. Anchises said that Augustus was a man of divine race who would establish a new golden age and extend the great Roman Empire as far as India, the Caspian and the Nile. Anchises declared that such greatness would be the fruit of Aeneas's actions if he settled in Italy.

It was a Roman's true destiny, he added, to rule over nations. The shield that Venus gave to Aeneas (see pages 124–125) before his combat with Turnus in Italy showed a pageant of all the great historical events of the future, culminating in Augustus's victory at the Battle of Actium. The poet remarks that Aeneas had no knowledge of the events depicted on the shield, but he revelled in their image as he lifted it up to his shoulder. Venus's gift of the shield echoes the action of the sea nymph Thetis who, in the *Iliad*, persuaded the divine smith Hephaestus (known to the Romans as Vulcan) to make a shield for Achilles (see page 96).

exhorted her to save him by creating a distraction to avert the duel. Juturna disguised herself as a Latin soldier and roused the Rutulians, leading them onto the battlefield once more.

Aeneas tried to call his men back, but was hit by an arrow and forced to retire. Turnus exulted at the sight of Aeneas's wound and charged across the field in his chariot, killing many Trojans. As the battle rolled nearer, and Aeneas's doctor despaired of removing the arrowhead, Venus magically healed the wound with a herb. At once, Aeneas surged forth at the head of his army and when Juturna saw him she remembered Juno's warning. Tipping Turnus's driver out of his chariot, she seized the reins herself and drove Turnus all over the battlefield, struggling in vain to evade Aeneas as he closed in for the long-awaited duel.

Amata, watching the chaotic movements from the city walls, thought that her favoured champion Turnus had been killed, and hanged herself in despair. Meanwhile, Turnus was tiring. He realized that the truce had been sabotaged by

A fresco from Pompeii shows Aeneas wounded in battle; Venus looks on anxiously. In some tellings of the myth, she rescued Aeneas's spear during his battle with Turnus when the weapon became stuck in a tree trunk.

his own sister and grew even more frightened. Finally, he was unable to hide any longer – and Turnus and Aeneas faced each other for the last time. Fate stood still because the gods, too, realized that the moment of resolution had come. Jupiter held up his scales and weighed the destiny of each man. He made the assembled gods, including Juno, give an undertaking that they would no longer interfere in the course of events.

First, Turnus struck at Aeneas, but his sword snapped in two. Understanding that fate was against him, he froze as if rooted to the spot. He felt the sensation of a person in a dream who wants to run, but whose limbs refuse to function. He could see no escape, but no way of attacking either; and he looked around in vain for his chariot.

In the moment that Turnus hesitated, Aeneas poised his fateful spear and hurled it with all his strength. It flew like a black hurricane, whistled through Turnus's armour and slashed open his thigh. The massive warrior sank to his knees, while the Rutulians let out a groan that echoed around the woods and hills. Humbled at last, Turnus stretched out his hand and accepted that Aeneas had won the right to marry Lavinia. He said that enmity between them should now end and begged Aeneas to send his body back to his father.

Aeneas hesitated, remembering his own father and touched by Turnus's words. He might even have spared his opponent's life, but then his glance fell on the familiar studs of the ill-fated belt of young Pallas. The sight filled him with blind anger and, seething with uncontrollable fury, he sank his blade deep into his enemy's chest. Turnus's limbs slackened and chilled. With a terrible moan, his life departed to the shades below.

Aeneas and Lavinia married and had many children. So says the *Aeneid,* all Romans have the blood of Troy running in their veins.

127

Romulus – First Builder of Rome

After Aeneas had triumphed over Turnus in single combat, he married the princess Lavinia and settled in Italy, founding the city of Lavinium in her honour. The local population and Aeneas's Trojan followers lived together peacefully and, over the years, became one people. But the conflicts that would give birth to the great city of Rome were not yet over.

Several generations after Aeneas's death, a quarrel arose among his descendants. Amulius seized the throne of Alba Longa – a city founded by Aeneas's son Ascanius – from his twin brother Numitor and sentenced Numitor's daughter Rhea Silvia to a lifetime of chastity so that she could not bear an heir. This judgement was later cited as the origin of the Vestal Virgins, priestesses who led the Roman worship of Vesta, the goddess of the hearth.

But by chance the god Mars saw Rhea Silvia when she came to draw water at a spring in his sacred grove and he made love to her. She bore him twin boys, Romulus and Remus. Amulius flew into a fury, threw Rhea into prison and gave orders for the babies to be drowned – but his men could not bring themselves to kill the infants and abandoned them on the bank of the river Tiber. A she-wolf who came to the river to drink found the pair, who stretched out their hands to her appealingly. She suckled them and they were later brought up by a shepherd.

Numitor is Restored to the Throne

In time the boys grew into strong young shepherds, who occasionally raided Numitor's herds to support their community. One day they were trapped by brigands. Romulus escaped, but Remus

Romulus and Remus, left to die by Amulius's soldiers, were nursed by a she-wolf. The powerful wolf is an Etruscan bronze from the 5th century AD; the babies are Renaissance additions.

was captured and brought before Amulius, accused of stealing Numitor's cattle. Amulius sent the youth to Numitor who, in questioning him, realized that Remus was one of his lost grandsons. He released the young man, who rejoined Romulus; together they organized a rebellion, killed Amulius and restored their grandfather Numitor to the throne.

Romulus and Remus decided to found a new city on the spot where they had been rescued by the she-wolf. But the same brotherly jealousy that had torn Numitor and Amulius apart now surfaced between Romulus and Remus. There are different accounts of the quarrel, but the end result was that Remus was killed.

The Rape of the Sabine Women

The new city was named Rome (in Latin, Roma) after Romulus. But the population was composed largely of men, and the shortage of women threatened its survival into the next generation. Romulus sent messengers to many local tribes proposing marriage alliances, but with no luck. Then he hit upon a plan. The festival of the Consualia was due to be held in Rome and big crowds from neighbouring areas were expected to attend. Romulus knew that the men of the Sabine tribe would bring large numbers of their womenfolk with them. He called all the Roman men together and told them what to do to solve their problem.

When the festival began, the men of Rome ran through the crowd and seized all the young Sabine women. Each man kept the woman he managed to grab, although some aristocrats had also marked out the most attractive women and hired squads to capture them. The Sabine men were forced to leave, shouting and cursing, and promising that they would have their revenge.

The women, too, were angry and determined to resist. But Romulus himself went among them, reassuring them that the Roman men would treat them with the utmost courtesy and consideration, and do their best to win their love. In time,

A glass cameo from AD20 shows Aeneas surrounded by his descendants Julius Caesar, Augustus, Tiberius, Livia and Caligula. Germanicus floats above the group.

especially as they began to bear children, the Sabine women grew to love their husbands and to enjoy their lives in Rome. Nevertheless their fathers, still furious, gathered an army to attack. They managed to enter the city and the Sabines and Romans faced each other for the decisive battle. The Sabine women, torn between love of the families in which they had grown up and their new-found love for their husbands and the fathers of their children, could not bear the prospect of what must surely follow. Tearing their clothes and loosening their hair, they ran into the midst of the two armies, begging them not to fight. Instantly the confrontation ended. The Roman and Sabine leaders made peace and the two communities were united into one state, with Rome as its capital.

IMPERIAL SUPERMEN

The Romans were attracted to the Greek hero-myths not just as good stories but also as parables of power. So when, with the establishment of the Empire, supreme authority became vested in one man, state propagandists looked to the tales for role models to boost the imperial image. While poets ransacked Homer in search of epithets to eulogize the emperors, sculptors turned to antique models to portray them in poses recalling Theseus or Achilles. Some even started believing the claims: Commodus (AD161–192) styled himself the Roman Hercules and gave public displays of his fighting skills.

Above: Commodus poses as Heracles with lionskin and club. When he carried his identification with the hero to the point of appearing naked in gladiatorial shows, his ministers judged him insane and had him assassinated.

Left: Rome's first emperor, Augustus Caesar (63BC–AD14) bestrides the world like a colossus in the huge 2m-high statue known as the Augustus of Prima Porta after the location of his wife's villa, where it originally stood. The sculpture is now in the Vatican Museums.

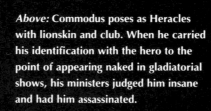

THE LEGACY OF THE HEROES

Few myths have proved as universal in their appeal as the Greek hero tales. Transcending the boundaries of space and time, the epics of Heracles, Jason and Odysseus find an audience today as readily as they did 3,000 years ago when the Bronze Age world in which they developed was drawing to a close.

Having survived the decline in Greek power and the rise of Rome, the myths faced their greatest challenge in the coming of Christianity, which replaced the worship of the classical gods as the official faith of the Roman Empire in the fourth century AD. With its emphasis on human imperfection and original sin, the new religion had little common ground with the legends. Tales of Perseus or Bellerophon could seem like the idlest of frivolities to proselytizers who were preaching the virtues of humility and turning the other cheek.

In addition the old stories, like all the classical heritage, were suspect because of their intimate connection with paganism. Hero cults had been common in many parts of the empire, and one central figure in the myths, Heracles, had been officially deified. One of St. Augustine's letters, sent to the inhabitants of what is now Sbiba in Tunisia, reproaches them for the massacre of sixty Christians; the occasion for the slaughter was the pulling down of two statues of Heracles, long worshipped in the town, on the orders of a Christian Roman Emperor.

Even so, official disapproval of the myths could not entirely kill off interest in stories so deeply important to the literature that educated people treasured. Ingenious ways were found to sanitize the tales for the new climate. One was to interpret them allegorically, re-reading the divine component as a series of metaphors for natural phenomena, chance, or the workings of the human psyche. Another was to rewrite the myths in such a way that the divine component was removed or reinterpreted in human terms. Two such retellings of the Troy legend were to have an enduring influence. Both were intriguing examples of that enduring genre, the literary fraud.

The first, an account of the downfall of Troy, purported to be the work of Dares, a Trojan priest who merits a passing mention in the *Iliad*. The second claimed to be a diary of the Trojan War kept by one Dictys, a Cretan accompanying King Idomeneus's contingent to the conflict. When interest in the classical world revived after the long sleep of the Dark Ages, the works of Dares Phrygius and Dictys Cretenesis, as the authors came to be known, became prime sources for several generations of authors.

The story of Troy was reinterpreted in a contemporary setting by the French 15th-century illustrator Raoul Lefevre, who imagined a turreted and castellated fortified city.

Jason sets out with the Argonauts in this 14th-century illustration from the *Historia Trojana* by Guido da Colonna. The voyagers are depicted as medieval knights.

The End of the Ancient World

But in the fifth century AD, when the surviving version of Dares's work was written, that prospect was still far away. As the classical world waned, the heroes for the most part shared the gods' fate, fading into semi-oblivion as literacy retreated and knowledge of Greek and Latin literature declined.

Yet even far from the classical heartland they were never entirely forgotten. Odd fragments of the old stories found their way, curiously distorted and transformed, into the legends of the peoples the Romans had traded with and conquered. Recently it has been suggested that the famous Cerne Abbas Giant, whose naked, club-wielding figure adorns a hillside in Dorset, England, may represent a folk memory of Heracles.

Some similarly antique tradition may have lain behind the claims made by Geoffrey of Monmouth in his *History of the Kings of Britain*, written in Latin in about 1135. Supposedly basing his case on "a most ancient book in the British tongue", he reported that the British nation had been founded by one Brutus, grandson of Aeneas

of Troy. In time the Trojan exiles were credited with establishing a city of Trinovantum, or "New Troy", on the site where London stood – a legend that apparently derived from the fact that a tribe called the Trinobantes had once lived there.

These tales became firmly established in medieval lore, forming a basis for one of the most popular romances of the early Middle Ages – the Jersey poet Wace's Anglo-French *Roman de Brut*. Adapted into English by Layamon in about the year 1190, this work was to be the source for a whole new epic cycle: the Arthurian legends.

The Myths in the Middle Ages

Other works were also reviving the Trojan saga, dressed up in the raiments of chivalric romance. As early as the mid-twelfth century, when knowledge of the classics was first reawakening, a cycle of verse epics known to scholars as the *romans d'antiquité* or "romances of ancient times" attained popularity in France. They included a *Romance of Thebes* and a *Romance of Aeneas*, both by unknown authors; but the work that attracted the most attention was the *Roman de Troie* by a French troubadour called Benoit de Sainte Maure. Benoit's work drew heavily on Dares and Dictys,

133

and it heightened the love interest in the original stories in keeping with the courtly tastes of the day. In the following century, it was to be rendered into Latin prose by an Italian scholar, Guido da Colonna, whose *Historia Trojana* would in turn inspire Giovanni Boccaccio, the author of the *Decameron*, and England's Geoffrey Chaucer.

In Britain the best-known medieval version of the tales was the *Troy-book*, a verse adaptation by John Lydgate, a monk from Suffolk. Completed in 1420, it incorporated many of the hero myths, starting with Jason's quest for the Golden Fleece and ending with the death of Ulysses. Lydgate's poem drew heavily on Guido da Colonna, and it was to be widely read for a couple of hundred years, providing source material for the dramatists Christopher Marlowe and William Shakespeare.

By the mid-fifteenth century the Renaissance was under way all across Europe, and the spread of Greek and Latin learning created the beginnings of a mass market for retellings of the classical legends. Significantly, the first book that William Caxton, who brought printing to England, chose to publish in his native tongue was a *Recuyell of the Historyes of Troye*; the second was a how-to guide to chess. He was a successful businessman, and he evidently knew where the tastes of fifteenth-century readers lay.

If the Middle Ages had for the most part interpreted the hero myths in their own terms, the Renaissance made more of an effort to recapture the true classical spirit – in part because of a better understanding of the original sources. Knowledge of Greek, which had died out in the West in the course of the Dark Ages, gradually spread once more, particularly after the fall of Constantinople to the

Turks in 1453 sent a stream of Greek-speaking scholars from the former Byzantium westward in search of a new home. With them they brought not only the language itself but also manuscripts that permitted scholars to read Homer and other poets in the original tongue.

The Renaissance took from the Greeks more than just the original plots of the tales. It also revived the concept of *arete* – excellence – which had always lain at the root of the heroic spirit. In quattrocento Italy, as in Pericles's Athens and the Rome of Virgil, a sense of human potentiality was in the air. The concept of the Renaissance man, master of every activity he tried, owed much to earlier Greek ambitions which found their purest

The quattrocento master Antonio Pollaiuolo was powerfully inspired by the legend of Heracles and painted him defeating the Hydra.

expression in the myths. At the same time, artists and sculptors learned once more to depict the ideal form of the human body. Masters such as the painter Andrea Mantegna and the sculptor Donatello copied Greek, or more often Roman, models to perfect the portrayal of musculature and of the look of limbs in motion. The myths themselves provided subject matter for masterpieces. The fifteenth-century Italian painter Antonio Pollaiuolo chose to depict *Heracles Fighting the Hydra* and the *Rape of Delanaira*, while a century later, the Dutch master of the nude, Peter Paul Rubens, painted a lusciously fleshy Andromeda and an action-packed *Battle of the Amazons*.

Faithful Penelope personified the 19th-century ideal of femininity. Here she is depicted by Edward Burne-Jones on a tile made by the William Morris Company.

Another achievement of the Renaissance lay in placing classical learning at the heart of education. Through the centuries that followed, a knowledge of the Greek and Roman authors was a fundamental part of any cultured person's store of background knowledge. In this way the hero tales became part of a universal language accessible to the lettered classes throughout the Western world.

As such, they proved endlessly attractive to poets, for whom the great classics served as touchstones of literary excellence. Some tested their talents against the originals by translating the major epics. In England, George Chapman showed the way in the 1610s with his pioneering versions of Homer's *Iliad* and *Odyssey*; 200 years later his translations were to inspire one of John Keats's finest sonnets. In 1697 John Dryden was to produce a rendering of Virgil's *Aeneid* in heroic couplets, and two decades later Alexander Pope did the same for both of the Homeric sagas. Pope also followed another established literary tradition

by using the classical epics as models for original works – in his case the satirical *Dunciad*, which adopts a mock-heroic tone to castigate Dullness.

Earlier masters had put the form to use in an attempt to create national epics. In France the *Franciade* by the great lyric poet Pierre de Ronsard was not regarded as a success, but Portuguese literature still saves a special place for Luis de Camoëns's *Lusiads*, a work of Homeric proportions whose central focus is Vasco da Gama's voyage around the world.

Dramatists also looked to the myths for themes for their plays. In France, Pierre Corneille's first tragedy was a reworking of the Medea story, taking its inspiration from Euripides, and he and Voltaire both produced versions of the story of Oedipus. Jean Racine began his career with *La Thébaide*, detailing the rivalry between Oedipus's sons, and his later works included dramas devoted to Hector's widow Andromache and to Iphigenia (drawing on Euripides's *Iphigenia in Aulis*) as well as to Theseus's wife in Racine's masterpiece *Phèdre*.

The Cult of the Hero

In the eighteenth century, the vogue for neoclassicism in the arts, inspired by the researches of the German art historian J.J. Winckelmann, renewed interest in the ancient world. It was left to the Romantics, however, with their obsessive individualism, to reinstate the cult of the hero in fully fledged form in such works as Keats's *Hyperion* and Shelley's *Prometheus Unbound*.

The developing demand for children's books in the nineteenth century provided a new audience for retellings of the tales. Well-known

135

authors including Nathaniel Hawthorne (in *Tanglewood Tales*) and Charles Kingsley produced versions of the legends for younger readers. Meanwhile, the Pre-Raphaelite vogue for fantasy stimulated adult interest in the stories. The poets Tennyson and William Morris both found inspiration for long poems in the hero myths, the first for his elegiac *Ulysses*, the latter for *The Life and Death of Jason*, which he also illustrated himself.

In the twentieth century, writers have shown a taste for dressing up the myths in a fresh guise, whether by retelling them in the light of a modern sensibility or else by using elements from them to add historical and cultural depth to essentially contemporary stories. In the latter vein, James Joyce's masterpiece *Ulysses* draws on the exploits of the Greek hero to provide structure and rich

irony to his tale of a day in the life of Leopold Bloom, an everyman who happens to be a Dublin advertising canvasser. In France, Jean Cocteau transferred the Oedipus theme to a contemporary setting in his play *La Machine Infernale*.

The *Oresteia* of Aeschylus proved very popular with twentieth-century authors. The French poet Paul Claudel translated it; Jean Giraudoux drew on it for his *Electra*. Eugene O'Neill preserved the Greek dramatist's trilogy format in *Mourning Becomes Electra* while translating the action to nineteenth-century America. Jean-Paul Sartre reworked it in existentialist terms in his wartime play *Les Mouches*.

French authors have in fact shown a particular enthusiasm for re-examining the Greek legends. André Gide wrote an *Édipe* and a *Thésée*, this

The Oedipus Complex

In modern times many writers have read psychological subtexts into the myths. No one took the process further than the founder of psychoanalysis, Sigmund Freud, who used the Oedipus story as the paradigm of each male child's love of his mother and jealousy of his father.

The Oedipus complex was central to Freud's view of human development. He thought that in early childhood a boy's nascent sexual desires are channelled towards his mother, and that as a corollary his first violent and aggressive impulses are directed at his father.

We are concerned with the hero's fate in the story, he wrote, "because it might have been our own, because the oracle laid upon us before our birth the very curse which rested upon him ... Like Oedipus we live in ignorance of the

desires nature has forced on us."

Freud's theory has since been modified or challenged by other psychologists. Carl Jung added the notion of an "Electra complex" to explain girls' affections for their fathers. Other writers have questioned the primacy that Freud gave to Oedipal feelings; but it was left to the British psychoanalyst Melanie Klein to point out that in many cases children's earliest aggressive instincts are in fact directed against their mothers.

The 20th century's greatest hero, Superman (Christopher Reeve), soars above a high-rise city in a still from the 1979 movie. Like the Greek heroes that his creators used as models, Superman is part human and part divine – an invincible being from the planet Krypton, but with the human capacity for love.

last his final novel. Besides his *Electra*, the novelist Jean Giraudoux had successes with *Amphit-ryon-38* – supposedly the 38th retelling of the tale of Heracles' mother's seduction by Zeus – and with *La Guerre de Troie n'aura pas Lieu* (The Trojan War will not Happen).

Superheroes and Superstars

Alongside intellectual interest in the myths has gone a revival in the realm of popular culture. Comic books in many languages have depicted the adventures of Jason, Perseus and Theseus in graphic, all-action detail. The twentieth century's own mythic hero, Superman, also owed much to his Greek predecessors; his creators, Jerry Siegel and Joseph Shuster, had Heracles very much in mind when they originally devised the caped crusader back in 1938.

The old stories also lent themselves well to cinematic treatment. In the 1950s and early '60s a series of Italian costume spectaculars, mostly starring a former Mr Universe, Steve Reeves, brought the stories of Heracles and the Trojan War to the screen in lurid colour. Hollywood followed this lead with a successful *Jason and the Argonauts*

featuring spectacular special effects by the master of the genre, Ray Harryhausen, and an inspired recreation of life among the gods on Mount Olympus. The myths attained a pop-culture apotheosis when Hercules was chosen by the Walt Disney Organization in 1997 as the subject for a full-length animated feature, following in the wake of such earlier heroes and heroines as Robin Hood, Pocahontas and Davy Crockett.

More artistically ambitious film productions included Pier Paolo Pasolini's extraordinary movie *Oedipus Rex* and Jules Dassin's updating of *Phaedra* to a modern setting. In *Orphée*, Jean Cocteau turned a recurrent personal obsession with the tale of Orpheus's descent into the Underworld into a haunting screen classic.

The sheer diversity of the uses to which the myths have been put confirms their adaptability as well as their universal appeal. Every age has reinvented the stories in its own terms and as a new millennium dawns they still seem fresh, showing few signs of their age. All the evidence suggests that the truths they tell about the human condition are timeless, and the legends might very possibly still be around to excite, enthral and terrify audiences in a further 3,000 years.

Index

Page numbers in *italic* denote captions. Where there is a textual reference to the topic on the same page as a caption, italics have not been used.

Picture Credits

Key: a above; **b** below; **c** centre; **l** left; **r** right

Abbreviations:

AAA	Ancient Art and Architecture Collection
AKG	AKG, London
AKG/EL	Erich Lessing, AKG
BAL	Bridgeman Art Library
CMD	Mike Dixon
ETA	e.t. archive
MH	Michael Holford
GDO	Giovanni dagli Orti, France

Title page AKG/EL; **Contents page** MH; **6** BAL; **7** CMD; **8–9** Robert Harding Picture Library; **9** GDO; **10** AKG; **11** CMD; **12** GDO **14** GDO; **15** GDO; **16** Roman Museum/Werner Forman Archive; **17l** Private Collection/Werner Forman Archive; **17c** GDO; **17r** Archaeological Museum, Naples/AKG; **18** British Museum/MH; **20** GDO; **21** AKG/EL; **23** Archaeological Museum, Thasos/ETA; **23** BAL; **24** Robert Harding Picture Library; **25** AKG/EL; **26** AKG/EL; **27** Capidomonte Museum, Naples/BAL; **28** Werner Forman Archive; **29** British Museum/MH; **30** ETA; **31** Louvre, Paris/BAL; **32** ETA; **34–35** Museo Archaeologico, Florence/Scala; **36** Werner Forman Archive; **37** Museo Archaeologico, Florence/Scala; **39** GDO; **40–41** Louvre, Paris/BAL; **42** Museo Archaeologico, Bari/BAL; **44** Museum Archaeology, Naples/AKG; **45** Louvre, Paris/AKG; **46c** AKG/EL; **46b** British Museum; **46–47a** AKG/EL; **47b** British Museum/MH; **48** British Museum/MH; **49** Glyptothek Munich; **50** CMD; **51** MH; **52** GDO; **54** CMD; **55** GDO; **56** MH; **57** Museo Pio-Clementino/Scala; **59** ETA; **60** AKG/EL; **61** Landesmuseum Oldenburg/AKG; **62** AKG/EL; **63** ETA; **64–65b** Archaeological Museum, Florence/Scala; **65** GDO; **66** AKG/EL; **67** GDO; **68** AKG/EL; **71** British Museum/MH; **73** British Museum/MH; **75** Archaeological Museum, Florence/BAL; **77** GDO; **78l** Capitoline Museum/Scala; **78r** AKG/EL **79al** National Museum, Naples/Scala; **79ar** British Museum/MH; **79b** GDO; **80** AKG; **81** GDO; **82** GDO; **83** Vatican Museum/Scala; **84** Archaeological Museum, Salonica/ETA; **85** AKG; **88a** Basel/AKG; **88b** Bonnat Museum/BAL; **89al** British Library/BAL; **89ar** Ducal Palace, Mantua/BAL; **89b** ETA; **90** Scala; **91** AKG; **92** BAL; **94** British Museum/MH; **96** ETA; **97** National Museet, Copenhagen/BAL; **99** British Museum/MH; **102** Villa Giulia, Rome/MH; **103** AKG; **104** AKG; **105a** Comstock; **105b** AKG; **106–107a** Bildarchive preussischer kulturbesitz; **106al** Bildarchive preussischer kulturbesitz; **106bl** ETA; **107ar** ETA; **107br** Bildarchive preussischer kulturbesitz; **108** Sonia Halliday Photographs; **109** GDO; **110** Archaeological Museum, Athens/ETA; **112** Gilles Mermet/AKG; **114** GDO; **115** BAL; **116** K&B News Photo, Florence/BAL; **118** The Hutchison Library; **120** AKG/EL; **121** AKG/EL; **123** AKG/EL; **124** AKG/EL; **125** National Museum, Naples/Scala; **126** Staatliche Glypothek, Munich/ETA; **127** Archaeological Museum, Naples/ETA; **128** Capitoline Museum, Rome/Scala; **129** Bibliotheque Nationale, Paris/ETA; **130ar** Capitoline Museum, Rome; **130b** BAL; **130bl** Vatican/Scala; **131** Vatican/Scala; **132** British Library/BAL; **133** British Library/BAL; **134** Uffizi/BAL; **135** Fitzwilliam/BAL; **136** Mary Evans Picture Library; **137** The Kobal Collection.

Further Reading

General

Calasso, Roberto (trans. Tim Parks) *The Marriage of Cadmus and Harmony*. Faber, London, 1988.
Cook, A.B. *Zeus*. Cambridge University Press, Cambridge, 1940.
Grant, Michael *The Myths of the Greeks and Romans*. Penguin, Harmondsworth, 1995.
Graves, Robert *The Greek Myths*. Penguin, Harmondsworth, 1955.
Hoffman, M. and James Lasdun (eds) *After Ovid*. Faber, London, 1994.
Hornblower and Spawforth *Oxford Classical Dictionary*. Oxford University Press, Oxford, 1996.
Morford, Mark and Robert Lenardon *Classic Mythology*. Longman, White Plains, New York State, 1991.
Rose, H.J. *Religion in Greece and Rome*. Harper and Row, New York, 1959.
Tripp, E. *Handbook of Classical Mythology*. Harper and Row, New York, 1970.
Warner, Rex *Men and Gods*. Penguin, Harmondsworth, 1952.
Willis, Roy (ed.) *World Mythology: The Illustrated Guide*. Simon & Schuster Ltd., London, 1993.

Greece

Aeschylus (trans. Robert Fagles) *The Oresteia*. Penguin, Harmondsworth, 1979.
Apollodorus *The Library of Greek Mythology*. Oxford University Press, Oxford, 1997.
Burkert W. *Greek Religion*. Blackwell, Oxford, 1985.
Buxton, R. *Imaginary Greece*. Cambridge University Press, Cambridge, 1994.
Carpenter, T. *Art and Myth in Ancient Greece*. Thames and Hudson, London, 1991.
Dodds, E.R. *The Greeks and the Irrational*. University of California Press, Berkeley, 1951.
Dowden, K. *The Uses of Greek Mythology*. Routledge, London, 1992.
Easterling, P.E. and John V. Muir (eds) *Greek Religion and Society*. Cambridge University Press, Cambridge, 1985.
Euripides (trans. Philip Vellacot) *The Bacchae and Other Plays*. Penguin, Harmondsworth, 1973.
Euripides (trans. Philip Vellacot) *Medea and Other Plays*. Penguin, Harmondsworth, 1963.
Euripides (trans. Philip Vellacot) *Orestes and Other Plays*. Penguin, Harmondsworth, 1972.
Festingiere, A.J. *Personal Religion among the Greeks*. University of California Press, Berkeley, 1960.
Finley, M.I. *The World of Odysseus*. Penguin, Harmondsworth, 1991.
Graf, F. *Greek Mythology*. John Hopkins, 1993.
Guthrie, W.K.C. *The Greeks and their Gods*. Methuen, London, 1950.
Guthrie, W.K.C. *Orpheus and Greek Religion*. Princeton University Press, Princeton, 1993.
Homer (trans. E.V. Rieu) *The Iliad*. Penguin, Harmondsworth, 1950.
Homer (trans. William Cowper) *The Odyssey*. Everyman, London, 1992.
Kirk, G.S. *The Nature of Greek Myths*. Penguin, Harmondsworth, 1990.
Kitto, H.D.F. *Greek Tragedy: A Literary Study*. Methuen, London, 1961.
Lefkowitz, K. *Women in Greek Mythology*. Duckworth, London, 1986.
Mikalson, J.D. *Athenian Popular Religion*. University of North Carolina Press, Chapel Hill, 1983.
Mylonas, G. *Eleusis and the Eleusinian Mysteries*. Routledge and Kegan Paul, London, 1962.
Nilson, N.P. *A History of Greek Religion*. Clarendon Press, Oxford, 1949.
Otto, W. *The Homeric Gods*. Thames and Hudson, London, 1954.
Rose, H.J. *Handbook of Greek Mythology*. Routledge, London, 1990.
Scherer, M. *The Legends of Troy in Art and Literature*. Phaidon Press, London, 1963.
Sophocles (trans. Robert Fagles) *The Three Theban Plays*. Penguin, Harmondsworth, 1984.
Sophocles (trans. E.F. Watling) *Electra and Other Plays*. Penguin, Harmondsworth, 1953.

Rome

Dowden, K. *Religion and the Romans*. Bristol Classical Press, London, 1992.
Ogilvie, R.M. *The Romans and their Gods*. Chatto & Windus Ltd, London, 1969.
Ovid (trans. Mary M. Innes) *Metamorphoses*. Penguin, Harmondsworth, 1955.
Perowne, S. *Roman Mythology*. Newnes, Twickenham, 1983.
Rose, H.J. *Ancient Roman Religion*. Hutchinson, London, 1948.
Scullard, H.H. *Festivals and Ceremonies of the Roman Republic*. Thames and Hudson, London, 1981.
Virgil (trans. Jasper Griffin) *The Aeneid*. Oxford University Press, Oxford, 1986.